THE EAT LOCAL COOKBOOK

the eat local
COOKBOOK

Seasonal Recipes from a Maine Farm

by

LISA TURNER

foreword by

Eliot Coleman

Down East

ISBN: 978-0-89272-923-4

Library of Congress
Cataloging-in-Publication
Data available upon request.

Design by Jennifer Baum
Cover Design by Miroslaw Jurek

Front cover photograph by Miller/StockFood

Printed in the United States of America

5   4   3   2

Down East

Books • Magazine • Online
www.downeast.com
Distributed to the trade
by National Book Network

To my four best friends: Ralph, Maggie, Will, and Katie

contents

contents

foreword

If you shop at a farmers' market or purchase locally grown vegetables from a nearby food co-op, you are benefiting from the hard work of small farmers. They are people who truly care about the quality of the food they produce. If you join a CSA for a weekly share, you have the opportunity to get to know small farmers on a deeper level. The work they do is not easy, but they know it is important. These are the type of people you want to have growing your food. They are hard working, knowledgeable, sincere, and conscientious. They have a passion for growing food the right way, not only as a culinary delight but also for its superior nutritional value. In order to do that, they have to know all about the importance of soil organic matter, balanced mineral sources, soil aeration, careful irrigation, and proper seed variety selection. They have to know those things in order to produce superior-quality vegetables whatever the season of the year. During my farming career I have gotten to know many of these growers, and I am always impressed by their dedication. Lisa Turner is one of the best of them, and she has pioneered new crops and new techniques. Who better to write a cookbook than someone who really knows what it takes to create great food?

Eliot Coleman
Harborside, ME
March 1, 2011

introduction

My husband, Ralph, and I own Laughing Stock Farm in Freeport, Maine. We have been growing vegetables year-round here for fourteen years. We grow on about fifteen acres in the summer and in five greenhouses in the winter. (Ralph, the mechanical engineer, has our greenhouses heated with used cooking oil that is burned directly in specialty burners in the winter. This allows us a much wider range of winter offerings while still being "seasonal" than may be available in your local area, but for this cookbook I've stuck with the standard seasonal offerings.)

Ralph and I started gardening when we were in college and had an interest in how the world worked before the time of grocery stores and easy access to food. We had chickens for meat and eggs, dairy goats, and grew all our own vegetables, although I have to admit I ate more zucchini that first year than I ever did before or after. Growing vegetables as a hobby can be relaxing, fun, and save you money. Unfortunately, I took this fun hobby to its evil endpoint and decided to start a farm

But seriously, I loved the gardening and wanted to provide my kids with a childhood where their parents were around, but were clearly involved in work, being that everyone needs to work to get along in life, and a farm was perfect for that. The kids worked on the farm from when they were small into their teenage years, and occasionally come back to work on the farm now. They understand that people need to work to get money, and they understand that work is generally not easy. They also learned to love good food.

A few years ago we wrote a business plan and needed to develop a mission statement. Since farming is all about the taste, we decided to simply say, "to delight the palate." That's it. For us it's about producing—and eating—great-tasting food.

Learning to cook is an offshoot of gardening and farming. If you decide to garden, you will no doubt be inundated with one vegetable or another from time to time, and this leads to a lot of spontaneous creativity in the kitchen. The need for creativity increases if you choose to farm. You end up surrounded by large quantities and varieties of amazing-tasting vegetables, and you have a strong need to cook at home and cook what's available because, as with any start-up business, there's really no money for the extras in life, like going out to eat, and sometimes not even for the grocery store. Necessity being the mother of invention and all, it's a great incentive to learn to cook. Having really tasty ingredients readily available makes it a lot easier to have the results turn out to be really tasty, too. It's been particularly fun to watch my kids learn to cook, and to share recipes and ideas with them, or just to listen to the answers they give when you ask what they think of a new dish and see how their tastes have developed.

When we started the farm, one of the ways we started selling was through a CSA, the abbreviation for Community Supported Agriculture, a sales program in which customers buy a "share" of the farm for the season, and come get their vegetables every week, taking whatever is ready. This means that pretty much everyone will, at some point in the summer, be given a vegetable they've never cooked before, or perhaps never seen before, or maybe a vegetable they long ago decided they really don't like. This is a challenge, not only for the customer, but also for me as a farmer. They want to enjoy what they get, and I want to have happy customers. This lead to me coming up with some ideas for what to do with the different vegetables that customers could try and be successful with, to create good-tasting dishes. Farming for a living required that most of these be quick solutions, which seems to be the situation for many of us. Cooking is generally not an all-afternoon affair. The kids were deeply involved in this process, unbeknownst to them, as they and Ralph were the first testers for many of these ideas. The results of this work are the recipes in this cookbook—healthy, fresh, local food that is quick to prepare and tastes great.

Cooking is definitely something that improves with practice. Try a recipe, one of these or any others, and it may not turn out as you'd imagined it the first time you make it. You try it again, adjusting the heat a little when you cook it, or adding a little more salt or less oil, and it comes out more to your liking. You start substituting ingredients. Eventually, you read most recipes as a general guide for cooking something, and make it on your own. Then one day you look in the refrigerator and take out a seemingly eclectic set of ingredients and come up with something new and wonderful. When you start making up your own dishes, think about balancing the basic flavors, like sweet, sour, salt, and bitter. Something that's a strong bitter like endive needs a strong balance of sweet or salt or both to really enhance the flavors. The goal is to have everything on the plate taste better because of the other things on the plate. Throughout all your cooking experiences there will be mistakes, but it's not all that often that you make a mistake so bad that you throw it out. More often the mistakes are a starting place for getting it right the next time. The main thing is try! I hope you enjoy these recipes and go on to create many more of your own.

—Lisa Turner

why eat local?

The grocery store is unbelievably easy. There are tons of products available from all over the world, why would anyone give up all that choice and convenience to "eat local?"

From my point of view, the number one reason is for the taste. Fresh, local food tastes better, period. And we all want to eat more food that tastes good. Imagine if all the vegetables you ate tasted sweet and were full of flavor. Imagine your kids asking for more vegetables. That is the most important part of eating local. Wherever you get your vegetables, if you don't notice an improvement in flavor in most of what you're getting as compared to the grocery store, you're missing the most important part of the eat local experience.

And it's not just the vegetables. We've used butter from local farms for years. One time my son invited some friends over for what he referred to as a "paint ball soiree." These were middle school boys who could get good and hungry. Will asked me to make pancakes and sausage for lunch, which I did, serving local sausage, butter, milk, and maple syrup at the meal. One of the boys raved about the butter. I saw him again about six weeks later, and he asked me where I had bought the butter. Imagine that, six weeks later a twelve-year-old boy still couldn't forget the flavor of that butter.

Think about it for a moment. We'd all prefer moist, flavorful roasted chicken; ham with its own unique flavor from someone's best family recipe for brining and smoking; big fat mussels that are harvested only when they reach that full fat size; hamburger that's naturally lean because it's from a grass-fed animal; sweet milk with plenty of cream in it. You want to come over for dinner, don't you? Don't worry, you can have all this at your house, too.

There are lots of other important reasons to eat local. If you buy from a local family-owned farm, they will pay wages to people who live in your area. The farmers and their employees will all spend a good portion of that money in your area, and that just keeps the local economy healthy. Consider this example: the town where we farm and live, Freeport, Maine, has about 8,000 residents. If every one of them spent only $5 per week on local produce, that would mean $40,000 per week being returned to our community, otherwise known as the local economy. Over a year this amounts to about $2 million dollars that would stay here in our home town. It adds up fast.

If you buy locally, your food is traveling a shorter distance to get to you, and therefore requires less fossil fuel for transportation and is fresher. Produce loses vitamins as it sits in storage, so fresh food is healthier than food that has been shipped a long way. So, it's good for the economy, environment, and your health. Local food is a win, win, win proposition.

Another perk of shopping with a local farmer is that you get to know the person who grows your food. If you shop at the farm, you get to spend some time at the farm, maybe even picking your own vegetables in the fields. If you're a regular at a farm or with a farmer at a market, you'll probably get to know their other regulars, too, which starts to build into a community. And in spending that money with your local farmer you preserve the farm landscape that everyone likes to see. If a farmer is making money on their farm, there's no reason for them to sell it for development. So you get to participate in the best type of land preservation, supporting family-owned farms just by eating fabulous food.

If you're concerned about what is going into your food or the environment in your community, who better to ask about how your food is grown than your farmer or someone who works on the farm. Local is not synonymous with organic, so if that's important to you, ask. "Certified Organic" means that the grower has filed paperwork describing all their growing practices and has had a site visit and audit by an independent, third-party certifying agency that is authorized by the USDA. Many growers at farmers' markets claim to be organic these days. You've probably heard people say "We do everything organic. We're just not certified." If you choose to purchase organic products, the only way to be sure you are getting what you pay for is to stick with a certified organic grower. We know lots of good, conscientious growers out there producing great products even though they are not certified organic, so you should be able to find something that suits your ethics as well as your wallet. Whether you choose an organic or other commercial farm, buying locally gives you the best chance to know what you're really getting.

All this said, there are plenty of "foods from away" in this cookbook. Local foods are the preponderance of the foods, but I like olive oil and lemon juice and pepper and many other things that couldn't possibly be grown here. In my opinion, coffee and chocolate greatly enhance my life, and lobsters and blueberries will greatly enhance the lives of people in other places. Therefore trade is good. What doesn't make any sense to me is to send hard-earned money to buy apple juice from China (one of the major importers of apple juice) when I can get apple cider from only thirty miles away. Once we send the money away, it's hard to get it back, so it seems best to keep it here if you can get the same thing (only tastier) in your own neighborhood.

Vegetables can generally be purchased from a farm very nearby, but animals require a lot of open land and so meat and dairy products may need to come from a greater distance. Other products like grains, storage potatoes, and dry beans may also require a greater land base for the farmer to be able to make a living, and larger farms are more readily available at a farther distance from population centers. Fortunately, many of these crops are grown to be stored for a period of time, so travel time does not affect quality. I'd still rather spend my money with people in another part of my state or region than to send it halfway around the world if I have the choice. I'll save the international trade for things I want from halfway around the world, like cinnamon and nutmeg.

how to eat local

In most areas there are lots of local foods available, you just need to pick the best option for you. Below are some pros and cons of all the possible ways to buy local food.

Gardening

Even as a farmer who makes my living selling vegetables, I have to say that the best way to get local food is to grow it yourself. This book contains some gardening tips to help you avoid some of what I have found to be the most annoying pitfalls, but it's not a gardening book. There are many, many gardening books of all types on the store shelves. Pick one and get started. First, get a soil test and follow the recommendations that come with the results, then plant a few vegetables. There really is nothing like planting a seed, tending your plants, and eating the food you grew. I can't recommend this strongly enough. It's hard to grow all your own vegetables, so for most people this won't be the only way they get food. (At least not for a couple of years! Practice makes perfect!) You can find out what you like to grow, what you're good at growing, and just specialize in a few crops or go wild. Garden and be happy!

Community Supported Agriculture (CSA)

In a CSA, you the customer pay the family farm in your community at the beginning of the season for all your vegetables. In a CSA, you are likely to be getting vegetables at the best possible price because you are paying ahead and agreeing to take whatever is ready as the season progresses. The farmer gives you a weekly share of whatever is fresh and ready on the farm.

That's the fundamental concept, but there may be as many variations on this as there are farms. Farms have different lengths to their season, different pick-up days, or payment plans. Check the number of weeks the farms in your area will provide you with vegetables, and use the cost per pickup as part of your comparison. CSAs should be more cost effective for the customer because of the benefits of this system to the farmer.

Some farms offer no choice and simply make up your bag for you. Some set the product out for you to choose, which will take longer but gives you a little more control over what you get. This option allows you to select large or small potatoes or turnips, for example. Some farms give you some amount of choice as to which types of vegetables you take, like pick two of the five types of potatoes available this week. Some even allow you the full choice of types and quantities of vegetables using a debit system to keep track of your remaining share balance. Many farms include some pick-your-own vegetables, herbs, or even flowers in the share. Most of our members, and especially their little kids, really enjoy the time they spend wandering through the flowerbeds making their weekly bouquet.

Regardless of the variations from farm to farm, in a CSA, you are committing to shop with just one farmer for the bulk of your vegetables that season, so your choices may be limited compared to some of the other shopping options. If you like surprises and trying new types of vegetables, this is a good option for you. Some CSA members think it's Christmas every week when they open their bag.

Some CSA farms will allow (or require) you to trade your labor for vegetables. Some offer shares of meat, dairy, fish, or other local products along with the vegetables and some have those things for sale, while some just keep the focus on the vegetables. So you can see, there's a lot to think about and a lot of questions to ask to compare CSAs so that you can become a member of the one that fits you best.

Farm Stands

You may live near a farm stand, where your local farmer sells their product. This is a great option for many people, as you will generally have lots of choice. A farm stand is the most likely of any of the buying choices to buy additional farm products from other farmers, so you're the most likely to have a steady supply of things like corn or strawberries in season, sometimes grown by the owner of the stand, sometimes by another farmer. This may cause you to question your own definition of local, at what distance is it still local?

Stands tend to be open several days a week and therefore offer a lot more flexibility for shopping. Some stands do not have a refrigerated area, and this limits the types of vegetables that the farmer can offer, for example you probably won't find lettuce if there is no way to maintain its quality on a hot summer day. Some have enough refrigeration to offer meat and cheese, including frozen or processed items along with fresh vegetables.

Farmers' Markets

Many towns have a small farmers' market, and most towns of any size seem to have a large farmers' market. Some markets have popped up recently, while others have been going for many, many decades in the same location. You will find a variety of vendors of various fresh foods, frequently including meat, cheese, breads, and ready-to-eat products along with the vegetables. Some markets also have craft vendors, artists, and even musicians interspersed with the food vendors providing a festive atmosphere. You may find the most choice at famers' markets because there are the most farmers, but you may need to travel to get the full range of choices. In some markets the farmers travel a long way to get to the market, which again is something that may define your personal definition of local. Markets can be a lot of fun, but they can also be crowded, and sometimes parking is a challenge. They are a great choice for people who enjoy shopping and have the time to do so.

Health Food Stores

Most locally owned health food stores are committed to their local farmers and buy most of their seasonal produce from local sources, as well as carrying other local products like meat, cheese, and prepared foods. They are most likely open more days than any other source, and are an easy way to shop. The prices may be somewhat higher than other options because you are helping to pay for the staff and building that provide you with that amount of convenience. The large chains buy from some local farmers, although you do have to look a little harder to find the local produce amidst all their other offerings. Although the stores have a commitment to the farmers they work with, you may not feel the same connection that you would if you had a more direct contact with the farmer. Still, for the very busy person, this generally offers the most availability and ease.

Co-ops

You may be able to find a co-op in your area, a group of people who get together to make a collective wholesale order to a farm or farms. This is probably the best way to make new friends from the experience because it takes a lot of committed people to make these work well. Prices should be good, since farms should be able to offer wholesale prices, but you may not get as much of a connection to the farm as you might with other options. If there is no co-op in your area, talk to some friends and start your own. In most locations you will also be able to find a wholesaler who will sell the same packaged products you see in the health food store to your group. For some people the ability to get wholesale prices on a wide variety of products makes this the best option.

gardening basics

Throughout this book you will find gardening tips for specific vegetables. Here I've compiled a few general gardening tips to get you started. The best way to learn how to garden is to try. It can takes years—lifetimes—to perfect, but get your hands dirty and you're guaranteed to learn very quickly and have fun. Who needs perfection, anyway?

Lime: The most important thing to add to the garden is lime. (No, not the citrus variety. The pulverized stone kind.) When the pH of the soil is too low the other nutrients can be tied up in a non-soluble form and be kept unavailable to plants. The University of Maine will do a soil test for only $15 that will list how much lime and nutrients to add to your garden. The order form and soil test boxes are available from every County Extension Agent or from the University of Maine.

Lead: Lead was used in paints until as late as 1978. The paint had LOTS of lead; a lead paint chip can be as much as 30 percent lead. The paint was designed so that the outside layer would slough off the building to keep the paint looking white. Lead is a very dangerous element, and being an element, it will never break down. It is dangerous to eat (and will be taken up by plants) and dangerous to breath as dust. The soil test from the University of Maine will test for lead as well as pH and nutrients. If there is lead in your soil, the best thing to do is cover it with a six-inch-thick layer of good soil and plant grass or nursery stock and leave it alone. Don't do anything to stir up any dust, and don't eat any plants grown in it.

Fertilizing: Lots of people tell me, "oh, you're organic, you don't use fertilizer." Every grower needs to use fertilizer, but organic growers only use naturally derived fertilizers like rock powders, blood, bone, or feather meal. Get your soil tested and add enough fertilizer to meet your crops' needs for nitrogen (N), phosphorus (P), and potassium (K).

Compost: I often get questions about "organic compost." Organic farmers are required to use compost that has been heated to high enough temperatures often enough to kill most pathogens. This compost can be made of any materials that do not specifically contain a lot of pesticides or herbicides, for example, no lawn clippings from a lawn where weed control or pesticides were used. It can contain conventionally grown vegetables or manure from animals fed conventionally grown feed. At this time there is very little commercially available compost made from all organically grown materials, so don't worry about it.

Ground Preparation: Weeds are what wear us down as vegetable growers. Everyone can plant more than they can weed. Now that you have your garden started, go till up just as much area as you just planted. Keep tilling this new area all summer to get rid of weeds, and then plant in that side the second year. If you want to keep the soil organic matter high in the area for year two, plant successions of oats and keep tilling them in before they or any of the weeds make seeds. The second year it should be much easier to keep all the weeds out, and the garden should grow with very few weeds and provide a much more enjoyable gardening experience.

Start Early: Lots of vegetables can be planted in the spring as soon as the ground can be worked and long before the last frost. Beets, carrots, radishes, turnips, bok choi, chard, lettuce, mesclun, arugula, spinach, lettuce, and broccoli raab can all be direct seeded. With an early start you can have fresh garden vegetables by early June. To tell if the ground "can be worked," dig up a handful of soil and squeeze it together. If it sticks together in a tight ball it is too early; when it is ready it will fall apart like moist chocolate cake.

Seedlings: It's really hard to grow good seedlings in your house. There just isn't enough light coming in through the windows, and even with grow lights it's easy to start more seedlings than there are lights. I tried to start seedlings indoors for years and could never figure out why I had such terrible seedlings. When we built a greenhouse I was instantly able to grow beautiful seedlings, all because there was enough light. There are good quality seedlings available at your farmers' market or local garden center. They, rather than big box stores, are the most likely to have varieties that are good for your area. Also, they are all plant professionals and will take the best care of the seedlings and are the most likely to notice any disease or nutrient deficiencies and sell only healthy plants.

Planting Particulars: When you plant a seedling, it is important that you fully cover all the soil and the peat pot (if the seedling is in one) with the garden soil. If the potting soil is left exposed, the water will wick right out of the root ball and dry out the roots. Covering them completely prevents this.

Late Starters: Many vegetables can be seeded or set out as seedlings in April, but some plants will die if they get frost and should not be planted until after the last anticipated frost (traditionally considered to be Memorial Day here). These crops include tomatoes, eggplant, peppers, squash, cucumbers, pumpkins, melons, beans, and most annual flowers. You also need the soil to be warm for these crops. If you can walk around in the garden with bare feet, the soil is probably warm enough, for these crops.

Black Plastic: Some heat-loving crops are hard to grow here in the north. To get good peppers, eggplants, or melons, get some sheets of black plastic, bury the edges in the soil, and cut holes in to put your seedlings in the ground. The soil under the plastic will heat up and help these crops to grow faster and produce bigger fruits. Garden centers and seed catalogs sell a very thin black plastic in row-sized widths, which is a better choice than large sheets from the hardware store.

Floating Row Cover: Plants that are set out as seedlings can usually handle some flea beetles, but direct seeded crops like arugula, mustards, radishes, and turnips look pretty ugly after the flea beetles get to them. You can protect these crops by covering them immediately after seeding with a floating row cover with the edges buried all around the crop. This filmy white fabric is available from seed catalogs and at many garden centers. The option is just to live with holey greens; the flea beetles rarely kill the plants.

Container Plantings: Container plantings are fun to have, whether it's a patio tomato or cucumber or hot pepper, or a hanging basket of flowers. Containers dry out quicker than plants in the garden and should be watered every day. They cannot grow deep roots and draw nutrients from the ground, so they will need to be fertilized about once a month.

Annual and Perennial Flowers: If you are growing annual flowers they will begin to flower early in the summer. Pick off the old ones in their entirety (called dead-heading) so that they cannot make seeds and the plants will continue to flower all season, or cut some flowers and put them on the table with your locally grown dinner. On perennial flowers you remove the dead blossoms because they are no longer pretty in the garden, but they do not bloom a second time.

Keep planting: Don't stop planting! When one plant is finished, put something else in its place. Fast growing vegetables like greens, bok choi, or radishes can be planted through the middle of August.

Cover Crops: Cover crops are plants that are grown for the sole purpose of tilling back in to improve the soil, or to hold the soil over the winter. They add organic matter to the soil, can provide cover for the winter, and can help choke out weeds. Oats make a nice winter cover crop that will die over the winter and can easily be worked into the soil in the spring. Plant oats by August 30. Winter rye will last through the winter and continue to grow in the spring. It can get very big in the spring, so you'll want to be careful that it doesn't get longer than your mower can handle. Plant winter rye by September 30, or double the seeding rate after that date and plant as soon as possible. You will not have time to get a cover crop on late fall crops, but as long as you've gotten cover on whatever you can, your garden will be fine.

a few words to the cook

You'll see some ingredients used over and over. Here are some things to think about when shopping or when trying to substitute what you have for what is called for.

Extra Virgin Olive Oil — I buy a large tin of extra virgin olive oil, and that's the oil I use for almost everything. Extra virgin oil comes from the first pressing of the olives and has the highest levels of olive oil's healthy components. The recipes call for "olive oil," and you should buy the best quality oil you can afford.

Butter — I've been using local butter for years, and in my area it is only available as salted butter. There are a couple of recipes that specifically call for unsalted butter; all the rest assume salted. If you prefer to use the unsalted variety, adjust your salt additions accordingly.

Milk — I use whole, unpasteurized, unhomogenized milk. You should use whatever kind you prefer, the recipes will turn out just fine.

Parmesan Cheese — You can buy a block of Parmesan and grate it yourself, which will always give you the best results. On busy days, you may want to use grated Parmesan that comes in a tub in the cheese section, or the stuff in a jar in the grocery section. A few of the recipes call for freshly grated because it will really, really make a difference for those recipes, but freshly grated will improve your results in all the recipes.

Spices — It's nice to use freshly grated nutmeg or ginger, but the cinnamon sticks that we get are generally of a lower quality than the cinnamon that's already been ground, so stick with ground cinnamon.

Salted Water — If you have hard water (lots of minerals in it) you may want to salt the water you cook your vegetables in to help preserve the vegetables' color. Other than that, it's a personal choice.

Cooking Temperatures — These are a general guide. Your cooking times will vary depending on whether you use a gas or electric stove, the size of the burners on the stove, and the type of cookware you use.

Washing Vegetables — All recipes assume you have thoroughly washed the vegetables called for. In some cases specific instructions are included in the recipes, when necessary. For more vegetable specific preparation and storage instructions, see pages 159-167.

Spring

Appetizers 24

Salads 28

Side Dishes 32

Entrées 37

Desserts 47

spring | appetizers

Crab Cakes on Pea Shoots

Serves 4

Pea shoots are the first section of the pea vine to grow up through the soil in the spring. There's a little bit of stem and some leaves, and it's all tender and mildly pea-flavored and delicious. You can also use later side shoots off the main pea vine, as long as they're tender. This is a very easy appetizer to make, but it looks and tastes pretty fancy.

Mash in a medium bowl:
> 1/2 **ripe avocado**

Mix in:
> **6 ounces cooked crab meat**
> 1/2 **teaspoon lemon juice**

Make four little patties and cover well with:
> **Italian seasoned breadcrumbs**

Fry lightly in a frying pan over medium heat in:
> **2 to 4 tablespoons olive oil**

Fry each cake for 3 to 5 minutes per side until golden brown. Be very gentle when flipping them.

Place each crab cake on a small plate on a bed of:
> 1/2 **cup of pea shoots that have been washed and dried**

In a small bowl, mix:
> **3 tablespoons sour cream**
> **2 tablespoons freshly squeezed orange juice**
> **zest from** 1/2 **large orange**

Drizzle the orange topping on the crab cakes and serve.

Variations
- Use 3 tablespoons sour cream and 3 tablespoons orange juice concentrate as the topping
- Use mayonnaise instead of sour cream in the topping

Radish Sandwiches

Makes 8

Radish sandwiches sound unusual, but we have several CSA members who swear by them. I made some for a party in my French class and the teacher, who is from France, assured me that they are very French, so you can feel very chic when you make them. They make a cute little appetizer, and they involve zero actual cooking. So there are no excuses!

Cut into quarters:

4 slices good-quality white bread, like a homemade loaf or sourdough bread

Butter half the pieces with:

plenty of butter

Thinly slice (about 1/8-inch thick):

1 bunch of radishes

Discard the greens, or add separately to a salad. Arrange the sliced radishes on the buttered bread. Sprinkle lightly with:

salt

Top with the remaining pieces of bread and serve.

Baby Lettuce with Steak and Arugula Pesto

Serves 4

Baby lettuce is not just a young lettuce plant, it's actually a miniature lettuce. In general, smaller versions of a vegetable are ready earlier, and this is true for baby lettuce. If you don't see these, ask your CSA farmer or farmers' market favorite to try them next year. A good seed catalog will have several different varieties for you gardeners to try. The importance of the baby lettuce in this recipe is that the small leaves will have a rib that will give them just enough rigidity to hold the steak. If you can't find baby lettuce, you could substitute individual leaves of baby bok choi.

Wash, dry, and arrange on a serving plate:
   several individual baby lettuce leaves

Season:
   3 to 4 ounces steak

With:
   salt
   freshly ground black pepper
   garlic powder

Grill the steak until it is just rare, about 3 to 5 minutes per side for a ³/₄-inch thick steak, then slice it into thin pieces and arrange a piece on each lettuce leaf.

Top with:
   ¹/₂ to 1 teaspoon Arugula or Basil Pesto *(page 154)*
   a sprinkle of finely diced red onion

Hot Fried Turnips

Serves 4

Hakurei turnips are a fabulous little "salad turnip" from Japan. They are much milder than the standard purple-top turnips that you see in the fall. They are great either cooked or raw. They cook faster than a purple-top turnip. Raw, they have the same crunchiness as a radish, but are much milder and don't have the sharpness of flavor that sneaks up on you after you eat a radish. If you're not a radish fan, try hakurei turnips in place of them. We've converted a lot of people to hakureis over the years.

Slice into $1/2$-inch thick disks:

1 pound turnips

Fry the slices in a large frying pan over medium-high heat in:

2 tablespoons olive oil

Let the turnips get golden brown on each side.

Season with:

$1/2$ teaspoon salt

$1/4$ teaspoon freshly ground black pepper

2 teaspoons crushed red pepper flakes

Serve as an appetizer with toothpicks.

spring | salads

Pea Shoot and Nectarine Salad

Serves 4

East meets west with nice fresh spring pea shoots and Washington state nectarines. Nectarines are delicious but don't grow reliably in Maine, but lobsters don't grow in Washington state. Trading an excess of a particular crop or catch can enhance lives in both places, but shipping in pea shoots that we can grow here just sends our money out of state. Buy what you can from local producers, and enhance your table with a few imported items.

Wash, dry either in a salad spinner or by tossing in a clean dish towel, and place on a salad plate:

> ³/₄ **cup pea shoots**

Arrange on top of the greens:

> ¹/₂ **sliced nectarine or peach**
> ¹/₈ **cup sliced almonds**

Mix together in a small bowl:

> 3 **tablespoon sour cream**
> 2 **tablespoons freshly squeezed orange juice**
> **zest from** ¹/₂ **large orange**

Variations

◆ Mix 3 tablespoons sour cream and 3 tablespoons orange juice concentrate for the topping.

◆ Top each salad with 1 to 2 tablespoons sour cream or crème fraiche.

◆ Top the salads with Balsamic Vinaigrette *(page 152)*.

◆ Put ¹/₄ cup cooked crab or lobster on top of each salad.

◆ If pea shoots are still available later in the season, use strawberries or raspberries in place of half or all of the nectarines.

Arugula and Pancetta Salad

Serves 4

Arugula is one of those polarizing vegetables, not unlike our last few presidents, you love it or you hate it, no one ever seems to be neutral on the subject. Those of us who love it do so because it has a nice peppery bite to it. It is a strong flavor, and it will be spicier when grown in hotter weather. When using it in a salad, you need to balance it with other strong flavors or it will overwhelm everything else on the plate. This recipe is courtesy of one of my CSA members, Lesley Mansfield.

Heat in a frying pan over medium heat:
   1 to 2 tablespoons olive oil

Fry slowly until caramelized:
   ¹/₂ yellow onion, thinly sliced

Remove the onions from the pan and fry to a very light crisp:
   1 to 2 ounces pancetta or prosciutto

Meanwhile, wash, dry either in a salad spinner or by tossing in a clean dish towel, and put in a large bowl:
   ¹/₂ pound arugula

Toss with:
   2 to 3 tablespoons Balsamic Vinaigrette *(page 152)*

Mix in the onions and pancetta or prosciutto, then divide onto plates. Top each salad with:
   ¹/₄ cup freshly grated Parmesan cheese

Basic Mesclun Salad

Serves 4

Mesclun is a mixture of baby greens, and may include any of the following: lettuces, mustards, baby chard, spinach, beet greens, kale, endives, or mache. What's in it may vary from week to week, depending on what's available in the garden. If you're shopping at the farmers' market you can try mixes from different farms to find one you like. If you grow your own you can start with a mix from a seed company and then add other items if you want, or develop your own signature mix. The greens grow quickly, so you have several chances over the course of the summer to adjust the contents to suit you. You can use lettuce instead of mesclun in this salad, or a mix of the two.

Wash, dry either in a salad spinner or by tossing in a clean dish towel, and put in a large bowl:

> ¹/₂ **pound (about 1 large bag) mesclun**

Toss with:

> ¹/₄ **cup Balsamic Vinaigrette** *(page 152)*

Add more vinaigrette if desired and toss again. Place the dressed salad on 4 salad plates and top each with:

> **a sprinkle of very thin slices of red onion**
> **a sprinkle of crumbled feta**
> **a sprinkle of raisins**

Options include adding more or less of any of the salad toppings, adding a sprinkle of pine nuts, or replacing the feta with crumbled sardines.

 Mesclun: Garden catalogs love to talk about mesclun as being a "cut and come again" crop. That is accurate, but misleading. It can be cut, it will come again and be cut a second time, and then it's done. MAYBE you can get a third cutting, but it doesn't go on and on all summer. The greens in a mesclun mix have very short life spans and will start to go to seed very quickly, which makes the leaves tough and bitter. To truly have a reliable supply of mesclun or arugula greens all summer, plant new seed every two to three weeks.

Baby Bok Choi Coleslaw

Serves 4

This is a nice, light slaw with a delightful Asian feel. It's a very quick way to prepare a vegetable that may not be a household standard, and it goes well with many different meals. Baby bok choi is usually available very early in the season, certainly before cabbage, so this can substitute for the more conventional coleslaw in a meal that calls out for cole slaw, like fish and chips.

Mix in a medium bowl:
> 1/2 **cup rice wine vinegar**
> **4 teaspoons sugar**
> 1/2 **teaspoon salt**

Chop up:
> 1/2 **pound baby bok choi (about 3 to 4 cups of chopped bok choi)**

Add the bok choi to the bowl, toss, and serve. You can make this ahead and chill for a few hours before serving.

spring | side dishes

Sautéed Radishes

Serves 4

Usually you think of radishes as a vegetable that can be served sliced on a salad or on a plate of vegetables with dip. Here's an easy way to branch out and try them cooked courtesy of CSA member Libby Moore.

Remove the greens from the top of:
1 pound radishes with tops

Chop the greens and set aside. Trim the ends of the radishes, then cut them into quarters. Heat in a large frying pan over medium–high heat:
1 tablespoon butter

Add the radishes and sauté until just barely tender, seasoning with:
¹/₂ teaspoon salt

Remove the radishes to a plate and cover to keep warm. Melt in the frying pan:
¹/₂ tablespoon butter

And sauté until just tender:
2 garlic cloves, minced

Add the greens and sauté, stirring until wilted, about 2 to 3 minutes. Add the radishes back in, stir, and serve warm.

Beet Greens

Serves 4

Most people my age didn't grow up eating beet greens, but you get to my parents' generation and they are all about the beet greens. They show up as one of the earliest greens at the farmers' market or CSA in the spring, and they should not be overlooked. Here's two simple ways to serve them.

Rinse very well and chop into ¹/₂- to ³/₄-inch pieces, leaves, stems, baby beets and all:
1 bunch beet greens

Steam until tender, about 5 minutes, and serve topped with:

> butter
>
> coarse salt

If there are leftovers, put them in a container in the refrigerator with ¹/₂ cup of the cooking liquid and:

> ¹/₄ **cup balsamic vinegar**

Marinate overnight and serve them as pickled vegetables the next day. I always cook extra so I can have enough left to marinate. The pickled beet greens are an interesting topping for a salad. This quick pickling would work with big arugula or braising greens, too.

Garlic and Ginger Broccoli

Serves 4

The first President Bush, George H.W., rather famously disliked broccoli and would not allow it to be served in the White House or on Air Force One. Our son, age two and a half at the time, loved broccoli. Based on this, we decided he was destined to become a Democrat. This recipe probably won't change your politics, but it is an easy way to dress up broccoli, and may win over some of those who have not yet learned to love broccoli! You could also do this with cabbage, cauliflower, broccoli raab, or bok choi.

Steam until it turns bright green and is just barely tender:

> **3 cups chopped broccoli**

Meanwhile, heat a large frying pan and melt over medium heat:

> ¹/₄ **cup (¹/₈ pound) butter (this recipe really wants the sweetness of the butter, so don't substitute oil)**

Sauté until tender:

> **4 garlic cloves, finely diced**

Add, stirring until the bread crumbs are just brown:

> ¹/₂ **teaspoon grated fresh ginger or ground ginger**
>
> **2 tablespoons Italian seasoned breadcrumbs**

Add the broccoli, toss it all until the broccoli is coated, and serve.

 Button Heading Broccoli: *Broccoli will live through very cold temperatures, but if it's very cold when the plants are young the broccoli will not develop large heads, just small "button heads." Don't plant broccoli when temperatures will still dip below 30 degrees.*

Chard with Feta and Olives

Serves 4

This is a very easy recipe, but it is one of my family's favorites. My older daughter always started nagging me beginning in February to get the chard growing because she thought it had been much too long since fall when she had last had chard cooked with feta and olives. You can use any kind of chard, but pick one and use it because this is a must-try recipe.

Remove the stems from:

1 bunch chard

Chop the stems into 1/4-inch pieces. Slice the leaves into thin strips. Heat in a frying pan over medium high heat:

2 tablespoons olive oil

Add, and sauté over medium-low heat until tender:

2 to 4 garlic cloves, finely diced

Add the stems and stir fry for a minute or so. Add the leaves and stir fry until the greens just turn bright green. Turn off the burner and top the chard with:

1/2 cup crumbled feta cheese

1/4 cup pitted, chopped kalamata olives

Cover the pan and let it set for a couple minutes until the feta begins to melt.
Serve topped with:

freshly ground black pepper

Turnip Greens

Serves 4

Go southern! We live in New England and won't typically see this dish here, but we certainly grow turnips in New England and those turnips have greens. They're delicious, so go ahead and serve this with a drawl. You could also substitute collards or kale.

Hard boil:

2 eggs

For the novice, this means to put the eggs in a saucepan. Cover them with water. Bring the water to a boil, turn it down to a simmer for 10 minutes. Pour the hot water out of the pan and cover the eggs with cold water. When that cold water gets warm, pour it out and add cold water a second time. You may have trouble peeling the eggs if they are too fresh. As eggs sit, air enters through the shell and enlarges the space between the shell and the membrane just inside the shell. When there is a little more air in there, it is much easier to peel the egg. Local eggs tend to be very fresh, so you may want to leave some in the refrigerator for a week or two if you want to have some to hard boil.

Peel the eggs and set aside. Fry in a frying pan over medium heat until crisp:

4 slices bacon

Set the bacon aside and remove all but two tablespoons of the fat. Wash, dry, and chop:

greens from one bunch of turnips

Heat the 2 tablespoons of bacon fat in the pan over medium-high heat.

Add the turnip greens and sauté until tender, seasoning with:

½ teaspoon salt

This will take 3 to 5 minutes, but will take longer with collards or kale. The best way is to sample it as you're cooking. Remove greens to a plate and top with crumbled bacon and chopped hard-boiled egg. Top everything with:

2 to 4 tablespoons hot pepper vinegar

I usually just add a little of the vinegar from the jar of jalapeños in the fridge.

Snow Peas with Pancetta and Artichoke Hearts

Serves 4

There are three types of peas that farmers grow. Snow peas or pea pods are eaten as just the pod, like in Chinese food. Shell peas need to be removed from the shell to get the little round peas out, and the shells are too tough to be edible. Snap peas are pods that fatten out with a pea but you eat the whole thing, pea and all. They are delicious raw, but if you manage to get any of them home, you could try this recipe that comes from Riley Shyrock, the head chef at Street and Co. restaurant in Portland.

Heat a large frying pan over high heat and add:

2 tablespoons olive oil (enough to cover the bottom of the pan)

When the oil is hot, reduce the heat to medium and add:

1 ounce pancetta, diced

Cook the pancetta until it starts to crisp and the fat renders, (until the fat comes out of the pancetta). Remove the pancetta from the oil using a slotted spoon and add:

1 pound snap peas, stem ends snapped off
1 cup quartered artichoke hearts (the kind from a jar)

Turn the heat up to medium-high and sauté the vegetables until they start to brown. Add the pancetta back into the vegetables and toss to mix thoroughly. Season to taste with:

salt
crushed red pepper flakes

Plate and drizzle over the vegetables:

balsamic vinegar

spring | entrées

Broccoli Raab Pasta

Serves 4

This is an easy way to use broccoli raab (or other cooked greens) to make a quick meal. It's also an easy way to start eating unfamiliar vegetables. You could also make this recipe with broccoli, broccolini, kale, or collard greens. Who doesn't like pasta and cheese?

Cook according to package directions:

1 pound macaroni or penne

Chop into 1/2 - to 1-inch pieces:

1 pound broccoli raab (stems, leaves, florets, yellow flowers and all)

About two minutes before the pasta is finished cooking, toss in the broccoli raab. Continue cooking for another couple of minutes until the raab turns bright green. Drain the water and put the pasta and greens back in the pan. Stir in:

1/2 cup olive oil

1 cup grated Parmesan cheese

The hot pasta and greens, coupled with the oil, will make the Parmesan nice and gooey. If you want to make it a full meal, add:

1 pound sausage, cooked over medium-high heat until browned and cut into bite-size chunks

Thai Curry

Serves 4

If you like the curries at Thai restaurants, you can easily make them at home using curry paste and coconut milk, which are both available at some grocery stores, health food stores, or Asian markets. There are several different types of Thai curry. Red and green are the hottest. The panang, yellow, and masaman are somewhat milder, but can be harder to find. Basically, you make a stir fry, mix in the curry paste, and then mix in the coconut milk, and there you have it!

Heat a wok or large frying pan over high heat. Turn the heat down to medium-high. Pour around the sides and coat the pan with:

2 tablespoons peanut or olive oil

Do not let the oil smoke. Add and sauté until just barely tender:

2 to 3 garlic cloves, finely diced

Turn the heat back to high and add:

1 pound pork, beef, or chicken, cut into 1-inch cubes

Stir fry until cooked through, about 5 to 7 minutes. Remove the meat from the pan and add:

2 cups sliced vegetables like onion, carrot, pepper, broccoli, or cauliflower (about ¾ pound of vegetables)

Stir fry the vegetables for a couple minutes, then add:

1 bunch chopped chard, kale, or spinach

When the greens are just beginning to wilt, return the meat to the pan and add:

2 ounces (½ can or jar) curry paste, or to taste

Stir until the meat and vegetables are coated. Turn the heat to medium-low and add:

one (13.5-ounce) can coconut milk

Stir and heat the coconut milk through. Check for taste and spiciness and add more curry paste if you'd like it to be hotter. Do not boil. Serve in a bowl over:

rice, cooked according to package directions

Be sure to add plenty of curried coconut milk to each bowl.

Spinach and Cream Cheese Omelet

Serves 1

This is the absolutely best omelet, ever. It gives you one more reason to look forward to spring so you can have some nice fresh spinach and make this omelet. It's really good served with toast with apple butter.

Heat in a small frying pan over low to medium heat:

  1/2 **tablespoon olive oil**

Cook until caramelized:

  1/2 **red onion, thinly sliced**

Add:

  1/4 **cup sun-dried tomatoes (the kind packed in olive oil—if you use the dry kind, you need to rehydrate them in a little hot water)**
  1 cup chopped spinach (about 11/2 **ounces)**

Cook until the spinach is wilted, and remove all the vegetables from the frying pan. In a small bowl, scramble together:

  2 eggs
  1 tablespoon cold water

Pour the egg mixture into the frying pan. Top one side of the egg with:

  1**1/2 ounces of cream cheese in thin slices**

And the vegetable mix. When the uncovered half of the omelet is barely set, fold over the eggs and cover the vegetables on the other side. Cover the pan and cook over very low heat until the eggs are just set, about 2 to 3 minutes. Serve immediately.

Broccoli Raab and White Beans

Serves 4

This is a great way to serve broccoli raab, and can be supper, or lunch, or, in small serving sizes, appetizers. Broccoli raab and white beans give this dish a classically Italian feel. It comes from our CSA member Shari Broder.

In a frying pan, heat:
> 1 tablespoon olive oil

Add and sauté until tender:
> 2 garlic cloves, minced
> 1/2 bunch scallions, green and white parts, diced
> 1 1/2 cup chopped broccoli raab, (about 1/2 bunch)

Add and mix:
> 1 can cannellini or other white beans, drained

Mix in the beans and season with:
> salt
> freshly ground black pepper

Serve on:
> toasted sourdough bread

Calzones

Makes 6

Sometimes you get a calzone that is basically a pizza folded in half. I prefer these, with a nice cheesy ricotta and greens for the filling. You can serve it with some warm Tomato Sauce *(page 153)* or store-bought spaghetti sauce on the side for dipping.

Preheat the oven to 425 degrees. Prepare Pizza Dough *(page 157)* or just buy frozen bread or pizza dough and thaw.

To make the filling, chop and steam until bright green:

    1 pound spinach, broccoli, chard, broccoli raab, or kale
    (about 8 cups lightly packed)

Heat in a frying pan over medium heat:

    2 tablespoons olive oil

Add and sauté together until tender:

    4 garlic cloves, finely diced
    1 bunch scallions, both green and white parts, finely diced
    or ¹/₂ medium onion, finely diced

In a large bowl, mix the vegetables with:

    1 pound ricotta cheese
    2 cups grated mozzarella cheese
    ³/₄ teaspoon salt
    ¹/₄ teaspoon freshly ground black pepper

Break the dough into six equal parts and roll out into circles on a floured board. Place ¹/₆ of the filling on one side of each circle, fold over, and seal with fork tines, like a pie crust. Place on an oiled cookie sheet, brush the tops with olive oil, and bake for 15 to 20 minutes, until the tops of the calzones are golden brown.

Cream of Greens Soup

Serves 4

You can use spinach, arugula, broccoli raab, or whatever you have to make this soup. A good dinner for a cool spring evening. In the fall, make it with celery. I hadn't made this in a while and when I finally did make it again, my husband couldn't stop raving about it.

Chop and steam until just bright green:

1 pound greens

Set aside. In a large saucepan over medium heat, melt:

3 tablespoons butter

Add and stir continuously:

3 tablespoons flour

Gradually add, stirring continuously:

2 cups milk

Continue stirring until the sauce thickens slightly. Add the cooked greens and:

1/4 teaspoon salt

1/4 teaspoon freshly ground black pepper

2 cups grated Monterey Jack or mild cheddar cheese

Turn the heat to medium low. Stir until soup is thoroughly heated, but be careful not to boil it or the milk will separate. If you get it too hot you can stir in cold milk and it will come back together. I like it chunky, but you can blend the soup at this point, taking care when putting hot liquids in the blender! Remove the little inside disk of the blender top and cover it with a kitchen towel. This will allow the steam from the soup to escape safely. Serve with bread and butter, or Biscuits *(page 156)*.

Beet Green and Potato Pancakes

Makes 8

The greens have a very mild taste in this pancake, so it's a good way to start family members who have not yet learned to love cooked greens. You could use chard, broccoli raab, or broccoli instead of the beet greens. My husband likes these with ketchup, like a hash brown, and you could probably make them for breakfast.

Grate:

3 medium potatoes (about 2 cups grated)

Chop small:

1 bunch beet greens

Mix the potatoes and beet greens in a large bowl with:

2 eggs, beaten
1 teaspoon salt
1 tablespoon apple cider vinegar

Grate and set aside:

8 ounces cheese such as cheddar, Monterey Jack, or Asiago

Heat in a large frying pan over medium-high heat:

2 tablespoons olive oil

Make each cake by putting about 1/4 cup of the potato mix in the frying pan and flattening it out with the back of a spoon. Put about 1/8 of the grated cheese in the center of the cake and top the cheese with another 1/4 cup of the potato mix. Be sure to leave room between the cakes while frying them. Brown each side of the pancake over medium heat, then turn the heat down to low, cover, and cook for an additional 5 to 8 minutes until the cake is fully cooked and the cheese is melted.

Spinach Cannelloni

Serves 8

These cannelloni have filling that is green on one side and white on the other, so they are delicious and cute. To save time you could make this as a lasagna, which means you don't have to make all the little rolls of cannelloni. Or make it as stuffed shells in large pasta shells.

Cook, according to package directions:

2/3 **pound lasagna noodles (about 14 pieces)**

When the lasagna is cooked, drain it, fill the cooking pan with cold water, and put the noodles in the cold water. This will keep them from sticking together while they wait.

As the pasta is cooking, steam until bright green (about 3 to 5 minutes):

3/4 **pound chopped spinach, broccoli, or chard**

In a food processor, mix:

2 eggs
2 pounds ricotta cheese
1 cup grated mozzarella cheese
1/2 **cup grated Parmesan cheese**
3/4 **teaspoon garlic powder**

Remove the ricotta mix from the processor. Put the steamed spinach in and process until smooth. Put 1/3 of the ricotta mix back into the processor and mix it with the spinach until smooth.

Make the sauce. In a medium saucepan over medium heat, melt:

3 tablespoons butter

Add, stirring continuously:

3 tablespoons flour

Stir constantly and add:

3 cups milk

Cook over low to medium heat, stirring until the sauce thickens. Add:

3/4 **cup grated Parmesan cheese**

Continue stirring until the cheese is fully melted. Put about a half cup of the Parmesan cheese sauce in the bottom of a baking dish and spread it around. Preheat the oven to 350 degrees and start making the cannelloni.

Remove a lasagna noodle from the water and slice it into 3 equal pieces. Put 1 to 2 tablespoons of the spinach mix across the center of the noodle. Put the same amount of white ricotta mix alongside it. Roll the noodle so that you have a small tube, about 1- to

1¹/₂-inch diameter and about 3 inches long, which is the cannelloni roll. Set it, seam side down, in the pan. Continue to make all the remaining cannelloni rolls. Pour the Parmesan cheese sauce all over the rolls, using a spatula to spread it evenly. Top everything with:

1¹/₂ cups grated mozzarella cheese

Bake for about 25 minutes until the mozzarella just begins to brown.

Garlic Shrimp with Baby Bok Choi

Serves 6

Garlic and shrimp are awesome together, and the green olives and baby bok choi bring this dish together with a refreshing, light, spring feel. You will need to use frozen shrimp, as shrimp season here does not overlap with bok choi season, but I think the frozen ones work just fine. Make sure to avoid using the olives with pimentos in them. If you're having trouble, look in the Greek or Italian sections of the store.

Preheat the oven to 350 degrees.

Melt in a medium baking dish in the oven:

¹/₂ cup (¹/₄ pound) butter

Add and cook until just translucent (about 3 minutes):

5 garlic cloves, finely diced

Add and cook for another 3 minutes:

¹/₂ cup pitted and chopped green olives

Turn the oven to broil. Add to the baking dish:

1 pound peeled and rinsed Maine shrimp

Broil for about 3 minutes.

Add and toss with the shrimp:

3 cups chopped baby bok choi

Making sure the bok choi is fully coated with the butter. Broil the dish for an additional 2 minutes, until the shrimp looks opaque instead of slightly translucent. Serve over:

rice, cooked according to package directions

Ham, Cheese, and Asparagus Casserole

Serves 4

Asparagus is great just steamed and topped with Hollandaise Sauce *(page 158)*. But this simple casserole is a great way to incorporate it into a full meal. This is a very easy, very light and fluffy casserole that's good enough for company. It does need to be mixed the night before, but it is quick to prepare.

In a large bowl, combine:
> 2 cups milk
> 4 eggs, beaten

Add:
> 1¹/2 cups cubed bread
> 1 cup cubed sharp cheddar cheese
> ¹/2 cup fully-cooked ham cubes
> 1 pound asparagus, tough bases removed and snapped into
>   1¹/2-inch pieces (about 1 bunch)
> ¹/2 teaspoon freshly ground black pepper

Mix thoroughly. Cover and refrigerate over night.

Preheat the oven to 350 degrees. Butter a casserole dish and pour the mix into it. Bake for 1 hour, or until a knife stuck in the center comes out clean.

spring | desserts

Rhubarb Pie

Although you hear more about strawberry rhubarb pie, I grew up eating just plain rhubarb pie, without the strawberries. My brother now lives in Texas, where it's too hot to grow rhubarb, and he pays a lot every year to get enough rhubarb to make at least one pie. Rhubarb is a funny plant—the leaves are toxic and the stalks are very tart, but with some added sugar they make a great spring treat. This is my mother Betty's recipe.

Make Basic Pie Crust *(page 155)* or thaw two pie crust sheets from a pre-made package. Preheat the oven to 425 degrees.

Cut into 1-inch chunks:

2 pounds rhubarb

This should give you 6 cups of rhubarb. Put the rhubarb in a large bowl and mix together:

1 egg, beaten

1 cup sugar

¹/₄ teaspoon salt

4 tablespoons flour

Roll out half the dough on a floured surface and place in the pie shell. Add the filling and dot the top with:

2 tablespoons butter, thinly sliced

Roll out the other half of the dough and place it on top. With a knife, trim the edge of the dough to even with the pie plate. Dip your fingers in water and wet the edge of the lower pie crust. Flute the edge of the top and bottom layer. The water will help the crust to stick together. Poke holes in the top crust and brush it with milk to brown the crust. Bake for 40 to 50 minutes.

Vanilla Bean–Mascarpone Panna Cotta with Fresh Rhubarb and Orange Compote

Serves 12

This recipe comes to us from Brandt Dadaleares, pastry chef at Fore Street Restaurant in Portland. Panna cotta is my younger daughter's favorite dessert, around here we refer to it as whipped cream jello. Brandt's version uses mascarpone cheese with the usual heavy cream. Thankfully, if we carefully follow Brandt's directions, this is something we can all pull off at home!

Place twelve (4-ounce) aluminum foil ramekins (available at gourmet cooking stores) on a cookie sheet. Put in a stainless steel bowl and let sit until it is at room temperature:

> 1 1/2 **cups mascarpone cheese**

Place in a large bowl and add enough cold water to cover:

> **5 sheets gelatin**

(If you have trouble finding gelatin sheets, you can substitute with packets of gelatin. One packet of gelatin equals three sheets of gelatin. If you use packaged gelatin, skip this softening step and just sprinkle it on the liquid when it is time to add the gelatin to the cream and sugar mixture.)

Let the gelatin sheets bloom and soften, squeeze out the excess water, drain the water, and place the gelatin back in the same bowl. Reserve.

Split and scrape the seeds out of:

> **1 vanilla bean**

In a heavy-bottomed stainless steel pan, combine the scraped vanilla bean with:

> 3 1/2 **cups heavy cream**
> **1 cup sugar**

Bring to a boil over medium heat.

Add the softened gelatin to the cream and sugar mixture. Turn off the heat and whisk thoroughly. Let this mixture sit for a few minutes to ensure that the gelatin has been dissolved.

Using a pitcher, pour the hot cream/gelatin mixture over the mascarpone cheese and let sit for five minutes. Strain the mixture through a fine sieve and pour into each ramekin. Place the cookie sheet of panna cottas in the refrigerator and let them set for four hours until completely jelled.

To make the topping, in a large bowl, combine and let set for fifteen minutes:

> **1 pound fresh rhubarb cut into 1-inch pieces, cleaned under cold running water, and drained**

¾ cup turbinado sugar (natural-unbleached) or
   white sugar if you can't find turbinado

Meanwhile, remove the zest from:

2 oranges

Set the zest aside. Next, make orange supremes. Using a paring knife, cut off the top and bottom of the previously zested oranges. Place the oranges on one cut side. Slowly cut off the rind, removing all the remaining rind down to the flesh of the orange, slicing from top to bottom and removing ⅙ to ⅛ of the peel with each slice. Make sure there is no white pith remaining. Pith is bitter; no need for that. Now cut between each segment, removing just the edible orange from the membranes. Remove any seeds. Place the supremes in a bowl and set aside.

Heat a heavy-bottomed stainless-steel pan over high heat for about 4 minutes. When the pan is obviously wicked hot, pour in the rhubarb/sugar mixture and let it bubble and shake until the rhubarb begins to soften. Stir once or twice. Do not let the rhubarb discolor. It will cook very quickly. Add the reserved orange zest and remove from the heat. Add the orange supremes and cool the mixture in the refrigerator.

To plate the dessert, warm each panna cotta in a platter of warm water for a few moments to loosen them, then invert each ramekin onto a plate and top with the rhubarb/orange compote. Candied almonds rock with this dessert!

Strawberry Shortcake

Serves 6

I grew up eating strawberry shortcake made with those little dessert shells and whipped cream from a can. It was a revelation when I had it on biscuits with homemade whipped cream! Make the biscuits big and thick for this recipe, it may mean you need to bake them a little bit longer. You may end up with extra biscuits.

Make the Biscuits *(page 156)*, adding into the dry ingredients:

1 tablespoon sugar

Trim the stems, core, and cut in half:

1 quart strawberries

Make Fresh Whipped Cream *(page 158)*. Cut the biscuits in half and place two halves in each dessert dish, cut side up. Top with 2 to 3 spoonfuls of strawberries, followed by 2 spoonfuls of whipped cream.

Strawberry Pie

This is a little different, but it's truly delicious. Kind of a twist on strawberry shortcake.

Preheat the oven to 350 degrees.

In a food processor, crush:

8 ounces shortbread cookies

Mix into the cookie crumbs until thoroughly mixed:

3 tablespoons butter, melted

Remove the mixture from the processor and press it into a pie plate. Bake for 15 minutes.

Put in the food processor and puree:

1 cup strawberries, washed, cored, and quartered

In a small saucepan over medium heat combine the strawberries with:

1/2 cup sugar
1 teaspoon lemon juice

Cook for about 5 minutes, until the sugar is fully melted and mixed into the strawberries.

Meanwhile, in a small bowl mix together:

2 tablespoons cornstarch
1/2 cup cold water

Add the cornstarch mix to the saucepan and stir to incorporate. Cook, stirring constantly, until the sauce thickens.

Place into pie shell:

2 cups washed, cored, and quartered strawberries

Pour the sauce onto the fruit and chill completely. Make Fresh Whipped Cream *(page 158)* and spread it over the top of the pie before serving.

Variation
◆ Slice one large banana and place a layer of banana in the pie crust first, under the strawberries.

Summer

summer | appetizers

Tomatoes and Mozzarella (Caprese Salad)

Serves 4

This is another super-easy thing to make, but it's always a hit. It is also my lunch most days in the summer. Make it with some different colored heirloom tomato varieties for a really pretty plate and some different flavors within the salad. As much as I love red tomatoes, I do think that, for the most part, the colored ones are even better.

Slice and arrange on a plate:
   3 large tomatoes

Slice and arrange on top of each tomato slice:
   3 large balls of fresh mozzarella

Top each piece of mozzarella with:
   one basil leaf

Drizzle on top of everything a little:
   olive oil

And sprinkle it all with:
   coarse salt

Tying Up Tomatoes: To tie or cage, that is the question! The answer depends on what you want from your tomatoes. If you cage them, the tomato will stay in the cage and make a lot of leaves and tomatoes. Because it makes so many leaves, it may make tomatoes a little more slowly, but it will make a lot of them. The tomatoes will be shaded by the leaves and will ripen a little more slowly, but will not have any sunscald (yellow areas) from too much direct light. If you tie them to stakes and trim the excess shoots so that you have one straight stalk they will ripen much more quickly. You might try doing half in cages and half with stakes.

Raw Fennel

Serves 4

It doesn't get any easier than this traditional Italian method of serving fennel. This is a light, crunchy, delicious starter for a hot summer's night.

Thinly slice:

2 fennel bulbs

Arrange on a serving plate and serve with separate dipping dishes of:

salt
olive oil

Pickled Beets and Eggs

Serves 8

Here in Maine pickled eggs are sold in a jar on the counter of the corner store. My mother grew up in Pennsylvania, where hard-boiled eggs go in with the pickled beets. The beet juice seeps through the egg white and makes it a lovely purple color. These pickled beets and eggs are terrific for a summer picnic, or as a quick snack or meal addition from the fridge.

Peel, slice, and boil until tender, about 15 to 20 minutes:

8 medium to large beets (about 4 cups)

Combine in a medium saucepan:

1/2 cup apple cider vinegar
1/4 cup sugar
1/4 cup water
1/4 teaspoon salt
2 teaspoons whole cloves

Bring the mixture to a boil. Remove from heat and cool slightly. Put the mixture in a bowl and add the sliced beets and:

8 peeled hard-boiled eggs *(page 35)*

Cover and chill overnight. Serve cold.

Stuffed Tomatoes

Serves 6 to 8

This recipe is best when made with plum tomatoes, but it will work with other tomatoes, too. There are even some varieties of tomatoes that are considered "stuffing tomatoes," which are probably easier to find in a seed catalog than at a farmers' market.

Preheat the oven to 400 degrees. Cut in half and scoop out the center of:

6 to 8 plum tomatoes

Put the scooped-out centers in a bowl and add:

¾ cup Italian seasoned breadcrumbs

½ to ¾ cup crumbled feta cheese

Put the mixture back into the tomato halves and place them on a lightly oiled cookie sheet or in a shallow baking dish. Bake for 20 to 30 minutes and serve immediately.

> **Tomato Hornworms:** *There's nothing like plucking a ripe tomato from a vine in your own garden. Unfortunately, some pesky little creatures can get in the way. Tomato hornworms are a translucent, light green worm with white and red markings and grow to be as big as your finger. When you see the first one you may think it's a beautiful creature. After it chews the leaves, stem, and tomatoes on your tomato plant you will begin to see it for the evil spawn of Satan that it is! I've had people tell me they thought deer were getting into their tomatoes when really it was just the tomato hornworms. The word "deforestation" comes to mind if they are given enough time on tomato plants. Fortunately, they are easy to control with one spray of bacillus thuringiensis, or BT, which is available at your local garden center.*

summer | salads

Frisee Salad

Serves 1

Frisee is an endive, and hence is a bitter green—bitter in a good way, of course. It is another green that needs to be served with other strong flavors like the anchovies in this recipe, but also seems to go well with creamy things such as hard-boiled eggs or a bottled Caesar dressing. This is one of my favorite salads. I frequently make it for lunch and just build it right on the plate.

Wash, dry, chop, and fill a plate with a layer of:

frisee

Top the greens with:

1 to 2 hard-boiled eggs *(page 35)*, **chopped**
4 anchovies, chopped
¼ cup freshly grated Parmesan cheese

Drizzle on the top:

2 tablespoons olive oil
1 to 2 tablespoons lemon juice or white balsamic vinegar

Top the salad with:

freshly ground black pepper

Variations

♦ Make this salad with romaine lettuce, which makes it a Caesar-type salad.

♦ Use a creamy dressing like Caesar or blue cheese instead of the olive oil and lemon juice.

♦ Use blue cheese instead of the Parmesan cheese.

Coleslaw

My daughters and I love coleslaw. When we go out for fried clams we always try the coleslaw first and discuss and critique it like we were judges on a cooking show. This is the one we make at home. I like to have some in the refrigerator for snacking, because even with the mayo and sugar, it's still a relatively low-calorie dish.

In a large bowl mix:
> $1/2$ **cup mayonnaise**
> **1 tablespoon apple cider vinegar**
> **2 teaspoons sugar**
> $1/2$ **teaspoon salt**

Add:
> **1 cup grated carrots (about 1 medium carrot)**
> **3 cups thinly sliced or grated cabbage, green, savoy or**
> **either one mixed with some red cabbage (about $1/2$ a medium cabbage)**

Mix it all together. This can easily be made ahead and stored in the fridge for up to three days.

Variation
♦ Substitute red wine vinegar and honey for the apple cider vinegar and sugar.

Broccoli and Cabbage Worms: Those pretty white butterflies that fly all over the cabbage and broccoli plants lay eggs for imported cabbage worms that eat the plants. Most years they are a nuisance, and just eat a few holes in the cabbage or leave a few worms on the broccoli. My advice is to ignore them, they die when cooked. If they really bother you, get some BT from your local garden center and spray as directed for imported cabbage worms.

Greek Salad

Serves 4

I can't begin to count the number of times I've made this salad. This is one of my summer standbys, and I might as well not make it if I don't make enough for my daughters. It's so good that I would advise making it in large soup bowls. It's in the salad section, but you could just make this salad the meal. The recipe is for four salad-size servings.

Cut into chunks and place in a bowl:

4 medium tomatoes

Add:

12 to 16 kalamata olives
1/2 cup thinly sliced red onion
3/4 cup crumbled feta cheese

Toss the salad with:

1/2 cup olive oil
2 tablespoons balsamic vinegar
salt
freshly ground black pepper

Variation

• Add 1 cup lettuce or diced cucumber.

Green Beans with Warm Mustard Vinaigrette

Serves 4

This is an easy way to dress up green beans and makes a nice accompaniment to many summer dishes. You can use regular green beans, or the yellow wax beans, or the fancier *haricot vert*, which are a thinner bean that are even more flavorful than regular green beans. "Haricot vert" translates as "bean green" in French, and they are sometimes called French fillet beans. This recipe comes from Theda Lyden, the executive chef at Freeport's Harraseeket Inn.

Boil a large pot of lightly salted water and add:

1 pound fresh green beans with the ends trimmed

Cook until just crisp, 3 to 5 minutes, and drain well.

While the beans are cooking, heat in a small sauce pan over medium heat:

1 shallot, minced
1 tablespoon Dijon mustard
1 tablespoon balsamic vinegar
¼ cup olive oil
½ teaspoon salt
freshly ground black pepper

Stir constantly until the mixture is hot to the touch. Toss the dressing with drained green beans and add:

2 tablespoons chopped fresh dill

Serve immediately.

Cucumbers with Dill and Sour Cream

Serves 3

The wonderful thing about local cucumbers is that they are not waxed like the ones in the store. This means that you don't have to peel them. You still can if you're accustomed to seeing them that way, or try only peeling strips down the cucumber so you have dark green and light green stripes around the edges of the slices. This is a very light salad, in spite of the sour cream.

In a small bowl, mix:

3 tablespoons sour cream

2 teaspoons white balsamic vinegar

1 tablespoon finely diced fresh dill

1/2 teaspoon freshly ground black pepper

Cut the ends off, peel or don't peel, and slice VERY thinly:

1 cucumber

Peel and slice VERY thinly:

1/4 medium mild onion

Stir the cucumber and onion into the sour cream mixture, cover, and chill for about one hour. This cannot be made too far ahead because the juice from the cucumber continues to seep into the sour cream/vinegar mix and makes it too watery.

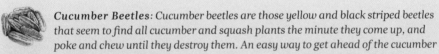

Cucumber Beetles: *Cucumber beetles are those yellow and black striped beetles that seem to find all cucumber and squash plants the minute they come up, and poke and chew until they destroy them. An easy way to get ahead of the cucumber beetles is to purchase seedlings that have their first true leaves (beyond the cotyledon leaves). These plants are generally big enough to handle some attacks by flea beetles and still grow into mature plants.*

summer | side dishes

Crunchy Kale

One of our CSA members, Shari Broder, shared this recipe and it got rave reviews from everyone all summer long. Imagine a bag of kale crunch next to the potato chips in the grocery store! Well, at this point you'll still have to make your own kale crunch.

Preheat the oven to 350 degrees.

Pour into a shallow baking dish and brush all over the bottom and sides:

    ¼ **cup olive oil**

Wash and chop into 1-inch squares:

    1 bunch kale

Put the kale in the pan and bake for 10 minutes, stirring once. Add and toss to coat:

    ¼ **cup grated Parmesan cheese**
    ½ **teaspoon salt**

Toss kale to coat it, and bake for another 10 to 15 minutes. Keep an eye on it and stir as necessary so it doesn't burn. Cool and store in an air-tight container.

Spicy Carrots

Serves 4

This is a completely different way to try carrots, and can be made as spicy as you and your family like. When you use the peeler or mandolin to prepare the carrots, you end up with lovely ribbons of carrot that get all coated with sour cream and spiciness. This is a fun little dish and would be great with either an Asian or Mexican meal.

Peel:

1 pound carrots

With the peeler or a mandolin, peel strips off the carrots, up to 4 inches long. Turn the carrot if the strips get wider than about 1/2 inch. You will end up with a core of carrot that you may not be able to peel.

Heat in a large frying pan over high heat:

1 tablespoon olive oil

Sauté, stirring constantly:

3 garlic cloves, finely diced

Turn the heat to medium, add the carrots, and stir fry them, stirring constantly for a few minutes. They will be very tender just because of the way they were cut. Add and mix in thoroughly:

2 teaspoons ground cumin

3/4 teaspoon hot sauce

Turn off the heat and stir in:

3 tablespoons sour cream

Serve immediately.

Carrots: Carrot seed is tiny and hard to plant at the final spacing that the carrots need to grow. Once the carrots come up, the plants need to be thinned to about two fingers apart. It might feel like you're hurting some of the plants, but if they don't have enough room they stay as tiny carrots and never reach a usable size.

Summer Squash or Zucchini with Garlic and Basil

Serves 4

There are many varieties of summer squash, patty pan, zucchini, and Lebanese squash. They can all be used interchangeably in any recipe. There are subtle differences in the flavors, but they all taste like squash. This is an almost instantaneous vegetable side dish. (And for the record, squash is also good served raw like a cucumber.)

Heat in a medium frying pan over medium-high heat:
>   **2 tablespoons olive oil**
>   **4 garlic cloves, finely diced**

Add and sauté quickly:
>   **4 small squash, very thinly sliced**

Add:
>   **4 tablespoons chopped basil**

Stir quickly and serve immediately.

Cucumber and Squash Successions: Cucumbers, summer squash, and zucchini plants have a life span, too, and don't go on all summer. To have these vegetables throughout the summer, make a second planting four to five weeks after the first planting.

Braised Fennel

Serves 4

Fennel can sometimes be hard to cook to a soft consistency, but this method will do the trick. If you're not sure you like the mild licorice flavor of raw fennel you should try it cooked, because the flavor becomes even milder. This is a simple, fool-proof recipe that comes from Ken Thomas, the sous chef at Fore Street restaurant in Portland.

Cut off and remove the stalks and reserve the fronds from:
> **2 fennel bulbs**

Chop:
> **1 tablespoon fennel fronds**

Cut bulbs lengthwise into $1/2$-inch slices, leaving the core intact.

Heat in a large frying pan over moderately high heat until hot but not smoking:
> **$1^1/_2$ tablespoons olive oil**

Add the fennel slices and brown well, turning over once, cooking for a total of about 3 to 4 minutes. Reduce the heat to low. Sprinkle the fennel with:
> **$1/_4$ teaspoon salt**
>
> **$1/_8$ teaspoon freshly ground black pepper**

Add:
> **$1/_2$ cup chicken stock**
>
> **$1/_4$ cup water**

Cover and cook until the fennel is tender, about 10 to 12 minutes. Sprinkle with fennel fronds and serve.

Egg Rolls

Makes 20

These are smaller than the ones you get at the Chinese restaurant. They are delicious, always well received, and a terrific way to use up any extra cabbage, which, let's face it, if you eat locally you're very likely to have! This recipe makes about twenty egg rolls, which is one package of wrappers. There's an easy dipping sauce you can make, too, so you don't have to use those ones in a jar, which are never as good as at the Chinese restaurant.

Filling

Heat in a large frying pan over medium–high heat:

>   2 tablespoons peanut, sunflower, or canola oil

When the oil is hot, lightly sauté:

>   1/2 medium to large onion, diced

Lower the heat to medium–low, add, and sauté for 2 to 3 minutes until opaque:

>   1 pound peeled and washed Maine shrimp

Remove the onion and shrimp from pan and add:

>   1 head savoy or Napa or regular cabbage, very finely sliced
>   2 large carrots, grated
>   2 medium turnips, grated
>   4 garlic cloves, finely diced

Add and toss:

>   4 teaspoons soy sauce

Cook until the vegetables soften. Remove the filling from the pan and make the egg rolls. In a very small bowl, mix:

>   2 teaspoons cornstarch
>   4 teaspoons cold water

Put two heaping spoonfuls of filling into each roll. Wrap as directed on the package, and seal with the cornstarch and water mixture.

Pour into the frying pan to a depth of 1 inch and heat on medium high:

>   peanut, sunflower, or canola oil

Test to see if it's hot enough by putting one egg roll in the oil. If it sizzles, it's ready. Put egg rolls in, seam side down, and fry until they are golden brown, about 2 to 3 minutes per side. Do not let them touch, or they'll stick together. Flip and fry the other side. Remove to a paper towel. Serve with dipping sauce.

Dipping Sauce

In a small saucepan over medium-low heat, mix:

6 tablespoons unsweetened applesauce

$1/2$ cup water

$1/2$ cup honey

2 teaspoons cornstarch

4 teaspoons prepared mustard

Stir until slightly thickened and serve with the egg rolls.

Green Beans with Shallot Horseradish Sauce

Serves 4

My older daughter says that green beans are best served raw, but if you decide to cook them (like most people do) you could try topping them with Hollandaise Sauce (page 158) or with this shallot sauce. If you can't find shallots, use one medium-size mild onion.

Trim the ends from, and steam:

1 pound green beans

Melt in a saucepan over very low heat:

2 tablespoons butter

Add and sauté until just soft:

4 shallots, minced

Add and cook until reduced by half:

$1/2$ cup sweetened wine like Madeira or sherry

Stir in at the end:

1 tablespoon prepared horseradish

$1/4$ teaspoon salt

If too much wine cooks away, just add a little more so that you have a sauce. Put the green beans in a serving dish, pour the sauce on top, and serve.

summer | entrées

Steak Salad

Serves 2

This has become a highly requested family favorite. It is also a delicious, easy meal to serve to company. If you have time to make a pickled vegetable ahead of time, like Pickled Beets *(page 53)*, you can use them, but if not you can use pickled red peppers or artichokes from the grocery store, or maybe another local pickled vegetable, like dilly beans or cauliflower from your farmers' market or local health food store.

Season:
> 12 ounces steak

With:
> salt
> freshly ground black pepper
> garlic powder

Grill the steaks to medium rare, about 5 to 7 minutes per side for a 1-inch-thick steak, and slice thinly.

Wash, dry, and place on a large serving platter or split onto two dinner plates:
> ¹/₂ pound lettuce or mesclun

Toss with:
> Balsamic Vinaigrette *(page 152)*

Top the greens with:
> ¹/₂ cup soft goat cheese
> 1 sliced tomato
> 1 cup sliced, pickled vegetable, like dilly beans, pickled red peppers,
>   pickled beets, or artichoke hearts

Top with steak slices and serve immediately.

Variation
◆ Top the salad with 1 cup cooked rice or orzo.

Cooked Cabbage or Lazy Stuffed Cabbage

Serves 4

There's a recipe for stuffed cabbage in the fall section, but summer is too busy to do that much work. This recipe starts as a side dish of cooked cabbage and onions and has optional add-ons that turn it into a one-pan meal: a "deconstructed" stuffed cabbage, as it were. I started calling it "lazy stuffed cabbage" and it turns out that's what it's called in Russia, too.

Heat in a frying plan over medium-high heat:
> **2 tablespoons olive oil**

Caramelize:
> **2 large onions, sliced**
> **4 garlic cloves, diced**

Caramelizing means to cook them until they are soft and browned and just starting to stick to the brown gooey layer that is building in the bottom of the pan. The point of this is that it brings out the sweetness in them.

Add and cook until wilted:
> **1 medium cabbage, shredded**

Add to taste:
> **salt**
> **freshly ground black pepper**

Variations

◆ Add 1 pound browned ground beef.

◆ Add 2 cups cooked rice and 1 pound browned ground beef.

◆ Add 1 large can of whole peeled tomatoes (or 3 large tomatoes sliced into wedges), 2 cups cooked rice, and 1 pound browned ground beef and now you've got Lazy Stuffed Cabbage!

Pan-seared Sea Scallops with Spinach and Corn Salad

Serves 6

Theda Lyden, the executive chef at Freeport's Harraseeket Inn, says, "This is one of my summer favorites that I often serve to friends and family so that I can enjoy the party, too. It's great served with a bubbly Prosecco." I concur.

Cook in a pot of boiling, lightly salted water:

> **6 ears corn**

Drain, cool, and cut the kernels off the cob.

In a large bowl, place the corn kernels and add:

> **6 cups (about 1/2 pound) spinach, stems removed**
> **1 pint cherry tomatoes, cut into halves**
> **1/3 cup basil leaves, thinly sliced**
> **3 scallions, white parts only, thinly sliced**

Mix together and season to taste with:

> **salt**
> **freshly ground black pepper**

In a blender or food processor, puree:

> **1 small shallot**
> **2 tablespoons balsamic vinegar**

While still blending, slowly add:

> **2 tablespoons hot water**
> **1 teaspoon Dijon mustard**

Very slowly, add:

> **1/2 cup olive oil**
> **salt**
> **freshly ground black pepper**

Toss the dressing with the salad and set aside.

Heat in a large frying pan over medium-high heat:

> **2 tablespoons olive oil**

Season:

1 1/2 to 2 pounds large scallops, muscles removed, with:

> **salt**
> **freshly ground black pepper**

Sear the scallops hard on one side so a nice brown caramelization occurs, about 2 to 3 minutes per side. You will know they are seared fully when they don't resist being turned over. If they are still sticking to the pan, wait a few more minutes.

Turn once and cook to desired doneness. You may need to turn the heat down to medium and continue to cook the scallops for an additional 1 to 3 minutes per side to fully cook the scallops once they are seared, depending on the size you can find. You will most likely have to cook the scallops in two or more batches. Be sure to allow the pan to become hot again before adding the later batches of scallops. You may need a little more oil.

Divide the salad onto six large plates and garnish with warm scallops.

Scallops are sold as bay scallops, which are relatively small, sea scallops, which are larger, but random sizes, and as sized sea scallops. If they say U–10, there are an average of ten scallops to the pound, which are very large scallops. U–20s have an average of twenty scallops per pound, and are therefore not as thick and will cook a little more quickly. They are done when you slice one in half and it looks completely opaque and flaky and there is none of the translucent quality of the raw scallop left.

Corn: *Corn is another delicious fresh treat that takes up a lot of room in a garden and is best avoided in very small gardens. If you do try some, it is important to know that it is wind pollinated and needs adjacent corn plants to get complete pollination and fill out the kernels. Plant at least four rows of corn to get adequate pollination.*

Oven-roasted Fennel with Fish

Serves 4

You can have just the fennel in this recipe, or add in a seasonal summer fish like bluefish or striped bass. You can just cook the fennel and serve it as an appetizer with a thinly sliced hard cheese such as Parmesan or Romano. This recipe comes to us from Riley Shyrock, the head chef at Street and Co. in Portland.

Preheat the oven to 350 degrees. Remove the tops and cores and slice in half lengthwise:

    4 fennel bulbs

Put the fennel in a large bowl and lightly toss with:

    zest of 1 lemon
    2 tablespoons white balsamic vinegar
    1 tablespoon ground fennel seed or fennel pollen
    1 teaspoon white sugar
    salt

Roast until just tender, about 45 minutes. Remove from the oven and drizzle the fennel to taste with:

    balsamic vinegar

Meanwhile, cut into 4 equal portions:

    1 to 1½ pounds bluefish or striped bass fillet, skinned and de-boned

Season to taste with:

    salt

Place the fish in a lightly oiled pan. Turn the oven to 500 degrees. When it's hot, turn it down to 350 degrees, put the bluefish in, and bake for 15 minutes, until it is just cooked but still moist and juicy. Remove the fish from the pan, place on a serving platter with the fennel, and drizzle lightly with:

    olive oil

Serve immediately.

Zucchini Casserole

Serves 6 to 8

Jordan's Farm in Cape Elizabeth has been growing vegetables for four generations and continues to be worked by members of the third and fourth generations. When I asked them to share a favorite recipe for this cookbook, Penny and her sister looked at each other and said at the same time, "Mom's zucchini casserole!" This was clearly a family favorite that their mother, Ruth Jordan, made. This casserole is great served with new potatoes and green beans.

Prepare Tomato Sauce *(page 153)* or use one (24-ounce) jar of prepared spaghetti sauce.

Preheat the oven to 350 degrees. Thinly slice:

1 large onion

3 to 4 medium zucchini

Pour about ⅓ of the tomato sauce into the bottom of a 2½-quart casserole dish. Place a layer of zucchini, then a layer of onions. Add another layer using half of:

2 pounds ground beef, crumbled

Put another layer of tomato sauce and cover with:

½ cup grated Parmesan cheese

2 to 3 tablespoons flour

freshly ground black pepper

Repeat the layers of tomato sauce, zucchini, onions, and ground beef, ending with the last of the tomato sauce. Top it off with:

1 cup grated Parmesan cheese

Bake for 1¼ hours until the hamburger is cooked and the zucchini and onions are tender.

> *Harvesting Squash and Cukes: Summer squash, zucchini, and cucumbers grow very quickly and it's easy to have them get away from you and get way too big. If they get over-grown they should still be harvested. If they stay on the plant it will start to put energy into completing the seed in the large vegetable. As gardeners, we need to convince the plant that it still has not made viable seed, and we do that by picking all the squash and cucumbers no matter how large they are. When annual plants make seed, they say, "my work here is done" and stop growing.*

Paella

Serves 2

Saffron is the magic ingredient that gives paella its unforgettable flavor. Saffron is the stigmas (little threads) from the center of the saffron crocus. People go through and harvest them as the crocuses open every day. Weird, but delicious, and it is definitely not an optional ingredient in paella. You can find this in the grocery store if you look hard in the spice section. It comes in a little vial or tin. Maine shrimp are only available frozen in the summer months, but they work just fine.

In your largest frying pan, heat over medium-high heat:

    3 tablespoons olive oil

Add and cook for about 5 minutes per side:

    2 to 4 pieces chicken, legs, thighs, or breasts

Remove the chicken from the pan. Brown:

    2 links chorizo

Remove, cut into chunks, and set aside. Preheat the oven to 350 degrees.

Dice small:

    1 cup of mixed vegetables, such as summer squash, peppers, carrots
      (1/3 to 1/2 pound)

Add carrots to the frying pan and cook for 2 to 3 minutes, then add squash and peppers and cook for an additional 1 to 2 minutes, but don't fully cook, and remove.

Add to the frying pan and quickly brown for about 3 to 5 minutes:

    1 cup arborio rice

To the rice add:

    1 cup chicken stock

Deglaze the pan by scraping the brownings off the bottom, which will be easy to do with the liquid you just added. Then add:

    1 cup chicken stock
    1/4 teaspoon saffron

Bring the rice, saffron, and liquids to a boil, then simmer for 8 minutes. Turn off the heat and add all the chicken, chorizo, and vegetables back into the pan, or transfer it all into a shallow baking dish and put it in the oven for 15 minutes.

Put in a bowl of water and cover with water to soak out the grit:

    3/4 pound mussels or clams

Drain the mussels or clams, then stir the paella and tuck them into the top of the rice along with:

> ½ **pound peeled Maine shrimp**
> ½ **cup shelled peas**

Return it all to the oven. Bake until the mussels or clams are slightly open, about 20 to 30 minutes. The lower portions of the rice will be moist, and the upper portion will be slightly crunchy.

> ***Peas and Snow Peas****: Peas fresh from the garden are a wonderful treat, but they do take up a lot of space for the amount of vegetables you get. If you have a very small space, these may not be the best choice for you to grow. If you do plant them, plant the seed very thickly. They can handle being close, and will give the best yields.*

Zucchini and Cheese Tart

Serves 4 to 6

Zucchini plants can definitely get ahead of you in the summer, leaving you wondering how to eat all they produce. This is a delicious and different way to use it. The recipe can be served as an entrée or side dish, and is good as cold leftovers for lunch the next day. This recipe comes to us from our CSA member Jen Galletta.

Preheat the oven to 350. Prepare half of the Basic Pie Crust *(page 155)*, or thaw one piece from a frozen package.

Heat a medium-size frying pan and melt over medium heat:

> 2 tablespoons butter or olive oil

Add and sauté until just tender:

> 1 medium zucchini or other summer squash, thinly sliced
>
> 4 to 6 scallions, both green and white parts, chopped
>
> 1 to 2 tablespoons chopped fresh herb mix such as rosemary, thyme, oregano, basil, or parsley

Roll out on a floured surface, place in a pie plate, and flute the edges of:

> 1 pie crust

Scatter across the bottom of the pie:

> 4 ounces blue cheese

Alternate layers of zucchini mixture and:

> 1 medium tomato, thinly sliced

Once the vegetables reach the top of the pie crust, bake it for 35 minutes. Let cool slightly before serving.

Spinach, Tomato, and Goat Cheese Quiche

Serves 4 to 6

Freeport has lots of bed and breakfasts, and our CSA members Tori and Robin Baron, owners of James Place Inn, shared this recipe from theirs. You can eat this quiche for dinner, or serve it for a very fancy breakfast and pretend you're on vacation.

Preheat the oven to 350 degrees.

Prepare half of the Basic Pie Crust *(page 155)*, or thaw one piece from a frozen package.

Heat in a medium-size frying pan:

> **1 tablespoon butter**

Add to pan and sauté lightly:

> **1½ cups chopped spinach (about ⅛ pound)**

Chop and set aside:

> **1 large tomato (about ¾ cup)**

In a large bowl, whisk together:

> **3 eggs**
> **¾ cup cream**
> **¾ cup milk**
> **½ teaspoon salt**
> **½ teaspoon freshly ground black pepper**

Roll out the dough on a floured surface and place it in a pie plate and flute the edges. Layer half the spinach into the crust, followed by half the tomatoes, then half of:

> **1½ cups crumbled feta**

Do a second layer of each item. Pour the egg mixture into the pie shell over the veggies and cheese. Bake for 40 to 45 minutes until a knife stuck in the center comes out clean. Let the quiche stand for 15 minutes before serving.

Variation
◆ Layer ⅓ pound cooked, crumbled bacon in the quiche to get a BLT flavor.

Basil Pizza

Serves 4 to 6

Growing up, pizza was dough with tomato sauce, mozzarella, and a choice of toppings. Lately the only commonality is the dough, and there's who knows what on top. I love the old kind, but pizza with fresh basil and fresh mozzarella is a whole different level of pizza, and is not to be missed.

Preheat the oven to 400 degrees. Prepare Pizza Dough *(page 157)* or just buy frozen pizza dough and thaw. Roll out the pizza dough on a lightly oiled board and place on a lightly oiled baking sheet. Bake the dough for about 10 minutes. Spread on top of the partially cooked dough:

> **2 to 3 tablespoons olive oil**

Cover the dough with:

> **³⁄₄ to 1 cup basil leaves**

Sprinkle lightly with:

> **¹⁄₄ cup freshly grated Parmesan cheese**
> **¹⁄₂ cup grated mozzarella cheese**

And top it all with:

> **3 balls fresh mozzarella cheese, sliced thinly**

Put pizza back in the oven until the mozzarella is gooey, but not necessarily brown, about 10 to 15 minutes.

Thai-accented Lobster and Native Corn Bisque

Serves 4

Usually I don't think of Thai and lobster in the same dish, but luckily Richard Lemoine, executive chef at Cape Arundel Inn in Kennebunkport, does. This is a truly delicious combination: lobster, vegetables, coconut milk, and Thai seasonings.

Cook in a pot of boiling, lightly salted water:

> 2 ears corn

Drain, cool, and cut the kernels off the cob and set aside.

In a large stockpot over medium heat, melt:

> 2 tablespoons butter

Add and sauté until fragrant, about 8 minutes:

> 1 small carrot, peeled and diced
> 1/2 red pepper, diced
> 2 stalks celery, diced
> 2 garlic cloves, crushed
> 2 teaspoons peeled and minced fresh ginger

Add and stir to make a paste:

> 1/2 cup flour

Slowly add to the paste, stirring constantly:

> 2 cups chicken stock
> 2 cups seafood or vegetable stock
> 1/2 cup sherry

Bring to a simmer and cook for about 20 minutes, skimming any foam off the top. Add:

> 6 basil leaves, chopped
> 3 tablespoons chopped cilantro leaves
> one (13.5-ounce) can coconut milk
> 4 tablespoons sweet chili Thai sauce
> a few drops toasted sesame oil
> salt
> freshly ground black pepper

Simmer for 3 minutes more and turn off the heat. Cool for 1/2 hour, then blend with a blender, food processor, or immersion blender. Put the soup back on the stove and add the corn kernels and:

> 2 cups lobster meat, cooked and chopped

Heat just through and serve.

Sausage and Kale Soup

Serves 4

This is a classic soup, also known as Portuguese kale soup. It is delicious, especially if you can find chorizo. Chorizo is a spicy sausage that is common in Portuguese, Spanish, and Mexican cooking and is available both fresh and dried (like pepperoni). Either type is great in this soup. Portuguese kale is actually a particular variety of kale with enormous leaves. It will be extremely difficult to find, so just use whatever type of kale you can find.

Cut into bite-size pieces and pan fry over medium-high heat:

1 pound chorizo or hot Italian sausage

Remove the cooked sausage from the pan. Add:

1 tablespoon olive oil

Gently sauté:

4 to 6 garlic cloves, finely diced

Add and sauté until just tender:

1 bunch kale, chopped

Add:

3 cups chicken stock

Add the sausage and simmer for about 20 minutes until it's all hot.

Variations

- Add 1 can cannellini beans or other white beans.

- Add 1 to 2 cups of cooked, diced potatoes.

summer | desserts

Apple Berry Pie

This is a fabulous summer dessert that gets rave reviews whenever I serve it. My kids make sure I freeze enough berries so that I can make it year-round. As with all pies, it's good served with Fresh Whipped Cream *(page 158)*.

Make ¹/₂ recipe of the Basic Pie Crust *(page 155)* or thaw 1 sheet of frozen pie crust. Preheat the oven to 400 degrees.

Peel, core, and thinly slice:

> **2 apples**

Measure how many cups of apples you have. Add:

> **strawberries, blueberries, raspberries, or blackberries (whatever mix you like, but at least two kinds to make up a total of 4 cups of fruit, including the sliced apples)**

Put all the fruit in a large bowl and add:

> **³/₄ cup flour**
> **3 tablespoons sugar**
> **¹/₂ teaspoon cinnamon**

Mix everything together. Roll out the pie crust on a floured board and place in the pie plate. Trim crust and flute the top. Add the apple/berry mix to the pie shell.

In a medium bowl, mix:

> **1 cup flour**
> **¹/₂ cup sugar**

Cut in with two knives or a pastry blender:

> **¹/₂ cup (¹/₄ pound) butter**

Sprinkle the topping evenly over the pie filling. Bake for 35 to 40 minutes.

Blueberry Buckle

This is a nice, light blueberry cake with a crumb topping and is one of my husband's favorites as it is his mother Lolly's specialty. You can also serve this as a coffee cake at breakfast.

Preheat the oven to 375 degrees. Place in a large bowl and cream together with an electric mixer until light and fluffy:

> ¼ cup (⅛ pound) butter
> ¾ cup sugar

Add and beat until smooth:

> 1 egg

In a medium bowl, sift together:

> 2 cups sifted flour (yes, it will be sifted twice—this adds fluffiness)
> 2 teaspoons baking powder
> ½ teaspoon salt

Alternate adding the dry ingredients to the butter and sugar with:

> ½ cup milk

Beat after each addition until smooth. Put in a medium bowl:

> 2 cups blueberries
> 2 tablespoons flour

Toss to coat the blueberries with the flour. The flour helps keep the blueberries from running and giving you a gray cake. Be gentle as you handle the berries. Fold the berries into the cake batter. Put the batter into a greased and floured 9"x 9"x 2" cake pan.

In a medium bowl, mix:

> ½ cup sugar
> ½ cup flour
> ½ teaspoon cinnamon

Mix the dry ingredients and cut in with two knives or a pastry blender:

> ¼ cup (⅛ pound) butter

Mix until it is crumbly and sprinkle evenly over the cake. Bake for 35 minutes, until a toothpick stuck in the middle comes out clean.

Blueberry Cobbler

This is kind of like blueberry pie filling with dumplings on top. Delicious! And even better served warm and topped with Fresh Whipped Cream *(page 158)* or vanilla ice cream.

Preheat the oven to 400 degrees. Heat over medium heat in a medium saucepan, stirring constantly:

> ¹/₂ **cup sugar**
> **1 tablespoon corn starch**

Stir in:

> **4 cups blueberries**
> **1¹/₂ teaspoons lemon juice**

Cook, stirring constantly, until mixture comes to a boil. Boil and stir for 1 minute. Pour into a greased 2-quart baking dish and place in the oven to keep it warm.

In a medium bowl, combine:

> **1 tablespoon sugar**
> **1 cup flour**
> **1¹/₂ teaspoons baking powder**
> ¹/₂ **teaspoon salt**

Cut in with two knives or a pastry blender:

> **3 tablespoons butter**

Mix in just until the dough forms a ball:

> ¹/₂ **cup milk**

Drop six heaping spoonfuls of dough onto the hot fruit. Bake for 25 to 30 minutes.

Blueberry Pie

Lots of people are afraid to make a pie, but the thing about pie is that even if it comes out runny or the crust is a little odd, you still have some great stuff to eat. And then you'll just have to try again to get it right. This pie is not hard, but if it doesn't come out perfect, then really, how bad is it?

Make one recipe of the Basic Pie Crust *(page 155)*, or thaw 2 sheets of frozen pie crust. Preheat the oven to 400 degrees.

In a large bowl, combine:

4 cups blueberries
¾ cup sugar
¼ teaspoon ground cinnamon
¼ teaspoon ground nutmeg
4 tablespoons flour

Roll out half the pastry dough on a floured board and put in a pie pan. Add the berry mixture. Dot the top with:

1½ tablespoons butter, thinly sliced

Roll out the second crust and place on top. With a knife, trim the edge of the dough to be even with the pie plate. Dip your fingers in water and wet the edge of the lower pie crust. Flute the edge of the top and bottom layer. The water will help the crust stick together. Poke holes in the top crust and brush it with milk to brown the crust. Bake for 35 to 40 minutes.

Maine Wild Blueberry Pecan Stuffed French Toast

Serves 8 to 10

One of my employees stayed at the Chadbourne House Bed and Breakfast in Eastport. David and Jill Westphal are the innkeepers and cooks there and make this stuffed French toast for their guests. My helper couldn't stop raving about it, and may have actually started to drool just a little bit as he described it. Many thanks to David and Jill for this recipe. Be sure to start this the night before you want to serve it. Another great breakfast or dessert.

Preheat the oven to 250 degrees.

Generously butter an 8"x 8" baking dish. Toast on a cookie sheet, 15 minutes each side:

1½ loaves firm-textured bread, sliced ½ inch thick

Remove and let cool (the bread will absorb the liquid better with this step).

In a medium bowl, mix:

one (8-ounce) package cream cheese
1 tablespoon wild blueberry jam

Spread the cream cheese mixture on half of the bread slices and place the other slices on top, creating a sandwich. Arrange stuffed slices in the buttered dish.

In a large bowl, whisk together:

10 to 12 eggs
1 1/2 cups milk
1 1/2 cups half & half
1/2 teaspoon grated nutmeg
1 teaspoon vanilla
1/4 cup packed brown sugar

Pour the mixture evenly over the bread. Cover the mixture with plastic wrap (pressing down to make contact and reduce air). Chill until all the liquid is absorbed by the bread, at least 8 hours or overnight.

Remove the dish from the refrigerator 1/2 hour before baking. Preheat the oven to 350 degrees.

In a shallow baking pan, spread evenly and toast until fragrant:

1 cup pecans, chopped coarsely
1 teaspoon butter
1/4 teaspoon salt

Increase the oven temperature to 400 degrees. Remove the plastic wrap. Sprinkle the pecans evenly over the bread mixture along with:

2 cups Maine wild blueberries

Meanwhile, melt together in a small pan and drizzle over the bread mixture:

1/4 cup (1/8 pound) butter
1/4 cup brown sugar

Cover the dish with foil. Bake for 30 minutes with the foil on top, then remove the foil for 20 to 30 minutes, until the top begins to bubble. Let stand for 10 minutes to allow the dish to firm up. Sprinkle with confectioner's sugar and serve with Maine maple syrup and/or Maine wild blueberry syrup!

Fall

fall | appetizers

Fried Green Tomatoes

Serves 6

People always ask what to do with green tomatoes. We like fried green tomatoes. I made them one weekend and found my younger daughter eating the cold leftover ones out of the fridge. She told me with a big smile, "these things are the bomb!" Apparently this is a good thing, and they really are very good. We went to a very fancy wedding in Charleston, South Carolina, in late June one year and they served fried green tomatoes at the reception.

Put in a dish:
> **1 cup flour**
> **$1/2$ teaspoon salt**
> **$1/4$ teaspoon freshly ground black pepper**
> **1 teaspoon garlic powder**
> **$1/2$ teaspoon paprika**

Scramble in a separate dish:
> **2 eggs**
> **2 tablespoons water**

Follow that with a dish of:
> **1 cup Italian seasoned breadcrumbs**

Slice:
> **3 large green tomatoes, about $1/4$-inch thick**

Dip each slice in the flour mixture, then egg, then breadcrumbs. The flour makes the egg stick and the egg makes the bread crumbs stick. On low to medium heat, fry the breaded tomatoes in:
> **$1/2$ to 1 cup olive oil**

Fry until the outsides are golden and the insides soft, about 3 to 5 minutes per side. Don't cook them too fast or the outsides will brown up before the insides are soft.

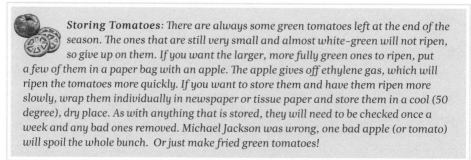

Storing Tomatoes: There are always some green tomatoes left at the end of the season. The ones that are still very small and almost white-green will not ripen, so give up on them. If you want the larger, more fully green ones to ripen, put a few of them in a paper bag with an apple. The apple gives off ethylene gas, which will ripen the tomatoes more quickly. If you want to store them and have them ripen more slowly, wrap them individually in newspaper or tissue paper and store them in a cool (50 degree), dry place. As with anything that is stored, they will need to be checked once a week and any bad ones removed. Michael Jackson was wrong, one bad apple (or tomato) will spoil the whole bunch. Or just make fried green tomatoes!

Updated Stuffed Peppers

Serves 4 to 6

These are best made with miniature sweet peppers, if you can find them. Or pick your peppers very small, or try a mild, round hot pepper. You could also quarter a full-size red pepper and put the stuffing in that. I don't do these as full-size stuffed peppers because the stuffing is rich and decadent. The kids are always thrilled when I make these.

Preheat the oven to 350 degrees.

Cut the tops off:

> **15 miniature peppers, or quarter 4 large peppers**

In a medium bowl, mix:

> **¹/₂ pound raw sweet Italian sausage, removed from casing**
> **4 ounces feta cheese**
> **³/₄ cup Italian seasoned breadcrumbs**

Add:

> **enough milk to make the filling into a sticky mess, about ¹/₄ to ¹/₂ cup**

Stuff the peppers with the filling and place them in a shallow baking dish. Fill the baking dish with water to half way up the peppers, or if you're using quartered peppers, just oil the baking pan and put them in. Bake for 20 to 30 minutes, until the sausage is fully cooked.

> **Hot Versus Sweet Peppers:** *Hot peppers are smaller and therefore will grow more quickly than bell peppers. They will do well without being planted in black plastic, but they will not get as hot when grown here as they do in Mexico or southern states. Less heat in the summer yields less heat in the pepper. To increase the heat, don't water them after about the beginning of September.*

Winter Squash in Filo

Serves 6 to 8

This involves filo dough, but don't be scared. The store-bought stuff is actually incredibly easy to use and the end product is very impressive. It reheats really well, too, so you can make it ahead and just heat it up for your event. You can also serve it in larger pieces as a side dish or dinner.

Thaw one package of frozen filo dough.

Preheat the oven to 375 degrees.

Cut in half and remove the seeds from:

> **1 large (or 2 small) winter squash**

Place the squash on a lightly oiled cookie sheet or baking dish. Bake until tender, about 30 minutes. Scoop the squash out from the skin and mash it. You need about 2 cups of mashed squash.

Mix in:

> **1½ cups ricotta cheese**

Set aside the squash mixture.

In a medium-size frying pan, over medium-high heat, melt:

> **2 tablespoons butter**

Add and sauté until caramelized:

> **2 medium onions, finely diced**

Add the onions to the squash.

In the frying pan, cook until brown, about 10 minutes:

> **1½ pounds crumbled sweet Italian sausage, casing removed**

Add the sausage to the squash mixture.

Turn the heat to low and melt:

> **1 cup (½ pound) butter**

Start layering the filo sheets into a shallow baking dish, brushing the butter between each sheet. Use six or seven sheets for the bottom crust, and top that with the squash/ricotta/sausage mix. Do another layer of about six or seven sheets of filo and butter, and then another layer of squash/ricotta/sausage mix. Put on the remaining filo sheets, still brushing the butter between each sheet. Brush the top with butter.

Bake for 45 minutes. Cut into pieces and serve. If you make it ahead, you can reheat it at 350 to 375 degrees until the filo puffs back up and it is heated through, about 10 to 15 minutes. They will reheat the quickest if they are cut into pieces.

Baba Ganouj

Serves 4 to 6

This is a Mediterranean dip that has a lovely smokiness from the eggplant and the toasted sesame seeds in the tahini. It's good for dipping vegetables or bread, or spread on Crostini *(page 156)*.

Preheat the oven to 400 degrees.

Put in a very small oven-proof dish:
> **1 full head of garlic, skin on**

Fill the dish ¾ full with:
> **olive oil**

Cut the stem ends off:
> **2 medium eggplants**

Poke holes in the skin of the eggplant with a fork, like you would for a baked potato. Put them directly on the oven rack, or on a cookie sheet to prevent getting drips on the floor of the oven. Bake the garlic and eggplants for 30 to 45 minutes, or until the eggplants are soft and look deflated. Put the garlic in to bake at the same time as the eggplant. The garlic will take less time than the eggplant, and is done when the cloves are relatively soft, about 20 to 30 minutes. Remove each when done, and cool. Scoop the centers out of the eggplant and remove the skin of the garlic. In a food processor, combine the garlic, eggplant, oil from cooking the garlic and add:
> **½ cup tahini (sesame-seed butter)**
> **juice from one lemon**
> **1 teaspoon salt**
> **½ teaspoon freshly ground black pepper**

Add more oil if the mixture is too thick to be a dip. Chill and just before serving, drizzle the top with:
> **olive oil**

Garlic: *Garlic will grow the biggest if you plant it in the fall. Cover it with about a six-inch layer of straw to protect it over the winter and keep the weeds out the following season. Use straw, which is the stems of grains like wheat or oats rather than hay, which is a grass plant, and includes the seeds on top of the grass. Using hay introduces more weed seed into your garden. Buy seed garlic from a catalog or garden center, not from the grocery store, as garlic in the grocery store may have been treated with chemicals to prevent it from sprouting. Break the garlic into individual cloves and stick into the ground as far as your fingers will go. Plant in a bed, with each clove six to nine inches apart.*

fall|salads

Old-fashioned Homemade Sauerkraut

Makes 1 gallon

Liz Sawicki, who is a cook at Street and Co. in Portland, makes sauerkraut from our cabbage every fall. Sauerkraut is traditionally eaten on New Year's Day with roasted pork, or served with hot dogs or on a Reuben sandwich. But it's good as a small accompaniment to other meals as well, so think creatively and enjoy a pickled vegetable, as pickles were made before the invention of canning.

Quarter and remove enough of the core to get the stem off:

5 pounds cabbage (2 to 5 heads, depending on size)

Thinly slice the cabbage and place it in a large bowl. As you are slicing the cabbage, sprinkle it with:

3 tablespoons sea salt or kosher salt (non-iodized)

This allows the cabbage to begin to release water as you're chopping. Once you have all the cabbage chopped, taste it for seasoning. It should taste a little salty at this point. If it doesn't just add some more salt. Let the cabbage sit for about an hour before you pack it. The salt will be drawing moisture out of the cabbage, creating the brine in which it will ferment.

Pack the cabbage into a one-gallon crock, pressing the cabbage down firmly as you fill it. When all of the cabbage is in there, place a clean plate on top and set a plastic gallon jug filled with water on top. There should be enough liquid to cover the cabbage by about an inch. Depending on the cabbage and time of year, it can take a little while for enough brine to be created to cover the cabbage. If there is still not enough liquid after a day, you can make your own brine by mixing together:

1 tablespoon sea salt or kosher salt (non-iodized)
1 cup water

Pour it on top until the cabbage is covered. Cover the crock with a cloth to keep out dust. Check on the kraut every couple of days to make sure the brine level is sufficient and to skim off any mold on the surface. Clean the plate and water jug as needed, and start to check the flavor after about two weeks. The sour flavor will intensify as it ferments. The kraut should smell sour. If at any time it doesn't smell delightfully sour, throw it out. After the kraut has worked for a week or two in the crock, it can be put into jars and stored in the refrigerator.

Kimchi

Makes 1 quart

Kimchi and sauerkraut are two ways to preserve cabbage for even longer than it can be stored under refrigeration. Kimchi is a Korean sauerkraut and is very pungent. It's definitely one of those flavor combinations that if you like you will end up craving.

Thinly chop or grate into a large bowl a mixture of:

> green cabbage
> savoy cabbage
> red cabbage
> carrots
> scallions

You should have about four cups total, which is about 1½ pounds of vegetables.

Add:

> 3 tablespoons freshly grated ginger
> 3 to 4 garlic cloves, minced
> 1 teaspoon crushed red pepper

Pound the vegetables with a wooden spoon or mallet. Put the mix into a wide mouth 1 quart jar and pack down. Mix together:

> 1 tablespoon sea salt or kosher salt (non-iodized)
> 1 cup water

Pour the liquid into the jar. Add more water if needed to just cover the cabbage. There should be at least 1 inch of space between the cabbage and the top of the jar. Cover tightly and keep at room temperature for about 3 days. After 3 days, store in a cool place. The kimchi can be eaten after 3 days, will develop more flavor in a week or two. As with sauerkraut, it should smell sour. Kimchi will smell more pungent than sauerkraut because of the ginger and garlic, but if it smells bad, throw it out.

Roasted Squash and Kale Salad
with Maple Garlic Dressing

Serves 4

This warm salad features great local fall ingredients. It has been a popular salad at Local Sprouts Cafe and is quick and easy to make, according to Jonah Fertig and Meara Smith, the recipe's originators.

Preheat the oven to 375 degrees.

Peel, remove and reserve seeds, and cut into 3/4-inch cubes:

1 medium winter squash

On a baking sheet, toss the squash with:

2 tablespoons olive oil
1/2 teaspoon salt

On a separate baking sheet, spread the reserved seeds and sprinkle with more salt.

Bake the seeds for 15 minutes, or until just golden. Bake the squash for 25 minutes, or until soft.

While the squash bakes, finely chop in a food processor or blender:

4 garlic cloves

Add and mix thoroughly:

1/4 cup Maine maple syrup
1/2 cup apple cider vinegar

Very slowly, drip by drip, blend in:

1/2 cup olive oil

Add:

a few sprigs of fresh herbs (parsley, chives, thyme), chopped

In a frying pan over medium-high heat, add:

1/4 cup water
1 large bunch kale, stalks removed and leaves chopped

Toss the kale and add more water as needed when the water evaporates. When the kale starts to soften, add the squash and toss. Remove from the burner and drizzle on the dressing. Put the salad into 4 bowls. Top with the roasted squash seeds and:

1/2 red onion, thinly sliced
salt
freshly ground black pepper

Serve immediately.

Arugula, Beet, and Feta Cheese Salad with White Balsamic Vinaigrette

Serves 6

Arugula is around for a long time, early spring right through mid-fall. This salad includes beets, which gives it the feel of autumn. You can make this salad with golden beets instead of red ones. Golden beets are milder in flavor than red beets, and have a taste halfway between red beets and carrots. They are a good starter beet for people who are sure they don't like beets. I like to think of them as a "gateway" beet. This recipe comes from John Shaw, the executive chef at One Dock Restaurant at the Kennebunkport Inn.

Boil until tender, about 30 to 45 minutes:

4 to 5 golden, red, or Chioggia beets

Cool, peel, and cut into bite-size cubes.

Whisk together in a small bowl:

1 cup white balsamic vinegar

¹/₄ cup sugar

¹/₄ cup Dijon mustard

2 teaspoons dried oregano

2 teaspoons dried basil

While whisking constantly, slowly add:

1¹/₂ cups olive oil

salt

freshly ground black pepper

Wash and dry with a salad spinner or pat dry with a paper towels:

1 pound arugula

In a large bowl, toss the salad with the beets and drizzle with the vinaigrette. Sprinkle the top with:

4 ounces feta cheese, crumbled

¹/₄ cup dried cranberries

¹/₄ cup toasted almonds

Celeriac Salad

Serves 4

This recipe requires cutting the vegetables into little matchsticks, also known as "julienne." The recipe comes from Sam Hayward, executive chef and owner of Fore Street restaurant in Portland, who recommends a Japanese mandolin for this purpose. If you don't have one, just cut the vegetables into matchstick-thin slices and then cut the slices into matchstick-thin strips.

Peel and julienne:

> 2 cups celeriac, a.k.a. celery root
> 1 medium tart apple like a Cortland or Liberty, cored

Julienne:

> 1 head Belgian endive

Combine the vegetables and apple in a salad bowl and toss well with:

> juice of one lemon
> sea salt
> freshly ground black pepper

In a small mixing bowl, combine and stir well:

> 1/3 cup mayonnaise
> 2 teaspoons cider vinegar
> 1 tablespoon stone-ground mustard
> pinch cayenne pepper
> 1/2 teaspoon fresh tarragon leaves, finely chopped

Add enough of the dressing to the celery root mixture to coat evenly. Taste for seasonings, and add, as necessary:

> salt
> freshly ground black pepper

Arrange on four salad plates:

> 2 cups fresh small-leaf salad greens, such as lamb's lettuce, miner's lettuce (claytonia), bok choi, young spinach, or a combination, washed and drained well

Spoon the celery root mixture onto the greens. Sprinkle over the salads:

> 1 tablespoon salt-cured capers, rinsed, drained, and coarsely chopped
> 1 tablespoon fresh chives, finely diced

fall | side dishes

Red Cabbage with Apples

Serves 6

Red cabbage is a vegetable we are most likely to eat as part of a colorful coleslaw, not as a stand-alone vegetable. That's too bad, because it is delicious and beautiful. This is an approachable dish to start your love affair with red cabbage.

Heat in a large frying pan over medium-high heat:
>   2 tablespoons olive oil

Add and sauté:
>   1 medium onion, sliced

Add:
>   1 medium head red cabbage, sliced
>   2 tablespoons apple cider vinegar
>   1 teaspoon sugar
>   2 large apples, peeled, cored, and chopped small
>   1 cup red wine
>   2 slices bacon, chopped into little squares
>   ½ teaspoon salt

Simmer for about an hour, until the cabbage is just tender. Serve warm.

Spicy Beets

Serves 4

This is one of David Iovino's best sellers at Blue Spoon in Portland where he is the owner and executive chef. He loves beets and has perfected some great ways to cook them. This is an easy method to try at home.

Preheat the oven to 400 degrees. In a large pot of water, boil until tender and peel:

    1 pound beets

Toast on a cookie sheet until just beginning to brown, about 10 to 15 minutes:

    1$^1/_2$ teaspoons cumin seeds

    1$^1/_2$ teaspoons coriander seeds

    1$^1/_2$ teaspoons fennel seeds

Grind the toasted spices in a food grinder, blender, or mortar and pestle with:

    $^1/_2$ teaspoon crushed red pepper

    $^1/_2$ teaspoon salt

Slice the beets and toss with spice mixture and:

    1$^1/_2$ tablespoons chopped fresh parsley

Serve at room temperature or slightly warm.

Variation

• Add crumbled feta cheese to taste.

> ***Frost on Root Crops:*** *If you are going to store some of your root crops, wait until after several frosts to dig them. The cold weather turns some of the starches to sugars, which gives you sweeter root vegetables.*

Mashed Potatoes and Kale

Serves 6 to 8

I thought I was quite clever when I had the idea to mix kale into the mashed potatoes, but it turns out it's the basis of a classic Irish dish called colcannon. Maybe Hamlet was wrong and the number of things on earth is limited. Regardless, it is a good combo.

In a large pot of water, boil:

2 pounds potatoes, chopped
3 to 4 garlic cloves, peeled

Simmer until the potatoes are tender, about 15 to 20 minutes. It's entirely up to you whether or not you peel the potatoes. If you want to have some additional texture in the final product, just be sure to cut the potatoes into fairly small chunks so that the pieces of skin are small. Drain and mash with:

3/4 to 1 1/2 cups milk
2 to 4 tablespoons butter

Meanwhile, heat in a large frying pan over medium heat:

2 tablespoons olive oil

Sauté until tender, about 10 minutes:

1 bunch kale, chopped

Mix the kale into the mashed potatoes and add:

salt
freshly ground black pepper

Variation

◆ Brown 1 pound crumbled sausage and mix with the potatoes and kale.

Potatoes: To grow potatoes, start with certified seed potatoes, not potatoes from the grocery store. Certified seed potatoes are carefully grown, starting only a few generations earlier with disease-free tissue culture. Samples of the seed potatoes for sale were grown out in Florida over the winter to make sure that no diseases that might be hidden in the tuber are expressed in the plant. There are many potato diseases, and one in particular, late blight, can travel 40 miles on a good wind. It will destroy all your potatoes in a week and then move on to the neighbor's house. Late blight is the disease that caused the Irish potato famine and is a real challenge even now for commercial farmers. Protect your own potatoes and those of the farmers in your area by using only certified seed potato.

Spaghetti Squash Tamales

Serves 4

I love spaghetti squash baked and served with just olive oil and Parmesan, but spaghetti squash are BIG and there tends to be a lot left over. This is a very different way to serve leftovers. Usually tamales are wrapped and steamed, but I lack the equipment to steam more than a few of them at a time, so these are baked. You can serve this as a side dish, an appetizer, or serve several for an entrée.

Preheat the oven to 400 degrees. Cut in half and remove the seeds of:

1 spaghetti squash

Place the squash cut side down in a shallow baking dish with $1/2$ inch of water. Bake for 30 minutes. Flip the squash and bake for an additional 20 to 30 minutes, until the flesh flakes out of the shell easily. You'll need two cups of flesh.

Meanwhile, heat in a large frying pan over medium–high heat:

1 tablespoon olive oil

Brown:

$1/2$ pound ground beef

Add and sauté until soft:

3 tablespoons finely diced onion
3 tablespoons finely diced green pepper

Add and mix in:

$1/2$ teaspoon garlic powder
$1/2$ teaspoon ground cumin
$1/4$ teaspoon salt
$1/4$ to $1/2$ teaspoon chili powder

Grate and set aside:

$1/2$ cup Monterey Jack cheese

In a large bowl, mix together:

1 cup cornmeal
2 teaspoons baking powder
1 teaspoon salt

Add the squash to the cornmeal and mix thoroughly with:

$1^{1/2}$ cups boiling water

Preheat the oven to 425 degrees. Place a sheet of parchment on a baking sheet. Put a heaping spoonful of the squash mixture on the parchment and spread it out. Top with a level spoonful of the meat and a large pinch of cheese. Top it all with a level spoonful of squash mixture. Squish the top layer down and seal to the bottom layer. Make additional tamales until you run out of components. Put them in the oven and bake for 20 minutes. Serve immediately with:

> **a dash or two hot sauce, if desired**
> **a small dollop sour cream, if desired**

Breaded Eggplant

Serves 2

This is a great side dish, but more frequently it's just my lunch. It's easy to do, and the Italian seasoned breadcrumbs have all the seasoning you need.

Slice:

> **1 eggplant**

Sprinkle both sides with salt and let set for 15 minutes to draw out the juices. Pat the eggplant dry with a towel. Dip the eggplant in water and then in:

> **Italian seasoned bread crumbs**

Heat in a large frying pan over medium–high heat:

> **4 tablespoons olive oil**

Brown the eggplant on both sides. Turn heat down to low, cover, and cook until eggplant is soft, about 5 to 7 minutes. Add additional oil if it is needed to prevent sticking. Serve immediately.

Red Flannel Hash

Serves 4

Hash is usually made with corned beef, but this Latin-style hash from Joe Boudreau, executive chef at Havana South in Portland, uses chorizo, which spices it up delightfully.

In a pan of water, boil until tender:
> 1 large beet, peeled and diced

In a large frying pan over medium-high heat, sauté until just cooked:
> 7 ounces Spanish chorizo, sliced
> 1 Spanish onion, peeled and diced

Add and sauté for a few minutes:
> 1 large sweet potato, peeled and diced
> 1 large Yukon Gold potato, diced
> 1 large carrot, peeled and diced

Add and simmer, covered, until all the vegetables are tender:
> 1 cup chicken stock

Add more chicken stock if necessary. Remove cover and simmer until nearly all the liquid has evaporated. Fold in the beets and season with:
> salt
> freshly ground black pepper

Variation
◆ Top with poached eggs and Hollandaise Sauce *(page 158)*.

fall entrées

Onion Soup

Serves 4

This is another incredibly easy dish, but it's delicious, and with the bread and cheese topping, it's also fun to eat. This is one that my younger daughter asks for on a very regular basis. Gruyere or Swiss would be traditional choices, but cheddar or Monterey Jack work really well, too.

Heat in a large saucepan over medium-high heat:

2 tablespoons butter

Add and sauté until caramelized:

4 large onions, sliced
4 garlic cloves, finely diced

Add:

4 cups beef broth
1 cup red wine
2 1/2 tablespoons soy sauce

With a wooden spoon, deglaze the bottom of the pan (remove the brown stuff that got stuck on the bottom of the pan). Add and simmer for 10 minutes:

1/2 teaspoon freshly ground black pepper

In a separate medium frying pan over medium heat, toast until golden brown:

4 thick slices baguette with both sides buttered

Put the soup into four oven-proof soup bowls. Top each with a slice of toasted bread. Top each piece of bread with:

1/8-inch-thick slice of cheese

Put the bowls on a cookie sheet to make it easy to move them and place under the broiler for about 5 minutes until the cheese is just melted.

Tuna Noodle Casserole

Serves 4 to 6

Yes, I know it's old school, but this is a little fancier version of tuna noodle casserole that's got a couple of interesting twists to it, including those awesome farm-fresh leeks and celery, so give it a try and be surprised. Maybe you can find a rerun of *The Brady Bunch* to watch while you eat dinner.

Preheat the oven to 350 degrees. Cook to al dente and drain:

1 pound macaroni, penne, or ziti

Heat in a large sauce pan over medium heat:

3 tablespoons butter

Add and sauté:

celery and leeks, chopped, a total of 3 cups, or about 1 pound

Add to the vegetables and stir for 3 or 4 minutes:

¼ cup flour

This butter and flour mixture can become lightly brown, but do not let it burn. Add and stir over low heat until it thickens:

2 cups milk

Mix in a large casserole dish or shallow baking dish:

2 cups shredded cheese (cheddar or Monterey Jack or a mixture of the two)
1 cup mayonnaise (yes, I said mayonnaise)
1½ cups white wine
1 teaspoon dill
2 cans tuna, drained

Mix the above ingredients, stir in the vegetable and white sauce mixture, and finally stir in the pasta. Sprinkle the top with:

½ to ¾ cup Italian seasoned breadcrumbs

Dot with:

2 to 3 tablespoons butter, sliced

Bake for about 25 minutes, until the top is just browned. I've started making this in a deep casserole dish rather than a shallow glass baking dish because everyone likes the topping and you get more of it that way.

Potato Leek Soup

Serves 4 to 6

If you serve this soup cold, it's vichyssoise. I like it hot because I eat it in the fall when the leeks are ready and you want a hot soup, and I call it potato leek soup. Either way, it's a classic way to serve a classic combination: potatoes and leeks.

Melt in a large pot:

3 tablespoons butter

Add and cook for about 10 minutes over medium heat, stirring enough so they don't stick:

4 cups thinly sliced leeks (about 1 bunch)

Stir in, cover, and cook for 10 minutes:

1 cup chicken stock

Add, cover, and cook for 20 minutes:

2 medium potatoes, peeled and diced
1 more cup chicken stock

Reduce the heat to a simmer. Stir in:

3 cups milk

Cover the pot and cook until the soup is heated through.

Add to taste:

salt
freshly ground black pepper

Let the soup cool a little and puree it in a food processor or blender. Once pureed, stir in:

1 cup heavy cream

Return to the pan and heat until just warm and serve.

Onions and Leeks: Onions and leeks take too long to grow from seed here, so you need to start with either seedlings or onion sets. Sets are little onions, and are available from catalogs and garden centers. Seedlings (the only option for growing leeks) are available from your local farmers' market, garden center, and occasionally from catalogs.

Stuffed Peppers

Serves 4 to 6

You probably ate these as a child. Isn't it time to give them another try? Yes, they're old school, but they are delicious. The cheese in the center is my mother's trick, and it's a good one!

Preheat the oven to 350 degrees. Cut the tops off and remove the seeds from:

4 to 6 green peppers

Boil a large pot of water and put the peppers in for 3 to 5 minutes just to soften them up.

Heat in a large frying pan over medium heat:

2 teaspoons olive oil

Add to the olive oil and sauté:

$1/2$ medium onion, chopped

Mix together the onions with:

1 pound raw hamburger
2 cups cooked rice, made according to package directions
$1/2$ teaspoon salt
$1/4$ teaspoon freshly ground black pepper
1 to 2 teaspoons Worcestershire sauce

Stuff the peppers with the hamburger and rice mixture and place them right side up in a shallow baking dish. Stuff the center of each pepper with a little chunk of:

Monterey Jack or cheddar cheese

Top each stuffed pepper with:

a spoonful of Tomato Sauce *(page 153)* **or store-bought tomato sauce**

With the peppers in the baking dish, add enough water so that it is about 1 inch deep. Cook for 45 minutes to 1 hour, until the peppers are tender and the ground beef is cooked.

Sausage, Peppers, and Onions in Cream Sauce

Serves 4

For the most part, my son just eats to stop being hungry, with little concern or apparent notice of what he's eating. This is one of the meals that he gets pretty enthusiastic about, as does the rest of the family. The creamy, garlicky wine sauce is absolutely delicious with onions, peppers, and sausage, and it's perfect over pasta.

In a heavy frying pan over medium-high heat, sauté:

> **1 pound Italian sausage, sliced**

Remove all but two tablespoons of the sausage drippings from the pan.

Add and cook until soft, about 10 minutes:

> **2 medium onions, peeled and sliced**
> **2 red peppers, cored, seeded, and sliced**
> **1 green pepper, cored, seeded, and sliced**
> **3 garlic cloves, finely diced**

Add:

> **1 cup white wine**

Cover and simmer until the wine cooks to half its volume. Add:

> **1 cup cream**
> **¹/₂ cup grated Parmesan cheese**

Cook over very low heat for a few minutes until the cream thickens. Serve over:

> **fettuccine or linguine, cooked according to package directions**

Moussaka

Serves 4

This recipe is from my brother, who spent a year in Greece when he was in the Air Force. My husband tells me that real moussaka has potatoes in it, but he bases this on the Greek restaurant he ate at in Alaska. I'm going with my brother's recipe, but it is just possible that in the thousands of years of Greek culture that they just might have developed more than one way to make it.

Peel and slice into ¼-inch slices:

2 large eggplants (about 1½ pounds)

Dust the eggplant with:

salt

And let set for 1 hour to draw out the juices and reduce the bitterness of the eggplant. Preheat the oven to 375 degrees. Heat in a large frying pan over medium heat:

1 tablespoon butter

Add and sauté:

½ medium onion, chopped

Add and sauté until brown:

1 pound ground lamb

Add and simmer for 15 minutes:

¼ cup dry white wine

¼ cup Tomato Sauce *(page 153)* **or store-bought tomato sauce**

1 tablespoon chopped parsley

¾ teaspoon paprika

¼ teaspoon freshly ground black pepper

1 teaspoon salt

Pat the eggplant dry with towels and dredge it in:

flour

In a separate large frying pan over medium to low heat add:

½ cup olive oil

Brown the eggplant in batches, about 5 minutes per side, adding more oil as needed.

Butter a casserole dish and coat the sides with:

Italian seasoned breadcrumbs

Place half the eggplant in a layer in the bottom of the casserole dish. Layer in the meat mixture followed by a second layer of eggplant. Top with:

> 2 medium tomatoes, sliced

In a medium bowl, beat together:

> 1 cup yogurt
> 2 egg yolks
> 1/2 cup flour
> 1/2 cup mild grated cheese (I usually use Monterey Jack. Not very authentic, but good.)

Spread the yogurt mixture over the top of the tomatoes. Bake for 45 minutes, until the topping puffs up slightly and is a very light golden brown.

Potato and Leek Casserole

Serves 4

This is like making those old family favorites, scalloped potatoes, but again, a little jazzier version with the leeks and some cheese. My kids definitely approve of potatoes made this way.

Preheat the oven to 400 degrees. Butter a large shallow baking dish. Layer the bottom with:

> 2 medium potatoes, thinly sliced

Add a layer of:

> 3/4 cup chopped leeks (about 1 medium leek)
> 1 cup grated cheddar cheese

Sprinkle the vegetables and cheese with:

> 1/4 cup flour

Dot with:

> 2 tablespoons butter

Repeat all the layers, then do one last layer of potatoes. Pour into the baking dish until it's 2/3 of the way to the top of the dish:

> milk

Sprinkle the top with:

> 1/2 to 3/4 cup Italian seasoned breadcrumbs

Dot with:

> 2 to 3 tablespoons butter, thinly sliced

Bake for 45 to 60 minutes until the potatoes are soft.

Polenta Lasagna

Serves 5

This fun variation on lasagna was developed by Abby Harmon, owner and executive chef at Caiola's Restaurant in Portland and her sous chef, Mike DeLosse. Instead of pasta, it features polenta, which is Italian cornmeal, and lots of tasty vegetables. You could make this with lasagna noodles, too.

Bring to a boil in a heavy stockpot:

> 4 1/2 cups water

Whisk in:

> 1 1/2 cups polenta or corn meal

Turn the heat to low. While stirring with a wooden spoon, add:

> 1/2 cup heavy cream

Let cook for about 10 minutes, until the spoon stands firmly in the polenta. Add water as necessary to get the appropriate consistency. Add seasonings to taste, including:

> salt
> freshly ground black pepper
> onion powder
> smoked paprika

Spread the polenta about 1 inch thick onto a baking sheet and cool in the refrigerator.

Meanwhile, in a large frying pan over medium heat add:

> 1 to 2 tablespoons olive oil

Sear for about one minute:

> 1 large red pepper, seeded and cut into 1-inch strips
> 1 large yellow pepper, seeded and cut into 1-inch strips

Add and cook for 3 to 5 minutes:

> 8 ounces button mushrooms, sliced

Add and stir for 30 seconds:

> 4 garlic cloves, minced

Add and toss:

> 2 cups spinach, chopped (about 3/8 pound)

Immediately remove the mixture to a bowl and toss with:

> 1/2 cup grated carrot (about 1 small carrot)

Add to taste:

salt

freshly ground black pepper

Heat in the frying pan over medium-high heat:

1 tablespoon olive oil

Add and caramelize:

1 medium onion, thinly sliced

Add the onions to the vegetable mix.

In a medium bowl, mix together and set aside:

6 ounces ricotta cheese

¼ cup flat-leaf parsley, chopped

⅓ cup grated Parmesan cheese

Mix together in another medium bowl and set aside:

⅓ cup grated Parmesan cheese

1 cup grated mozzarella cheese

1 cup grated provolone cheese

Cut the polenta into 4" x 5" squares. Heat in a large frying pan over medium heat:

¼ cup olive oil

Preheat the oven to 350 degrees. Pan fry the polenta squares, browning both sides, about 5 minutes per side. Place a square of polenta on a sheet pan and spread the ricotta mix, then add a layer of vegetables, and then a layer of mixed cheese. Place another piece of polenta, repeat the ricotta, vegetables, and cheese layers, and top with a final piece of polenta. Top with cheese mixture. Bake for 20 to 30 minutes, until bubbly and golden.

Pork Chops with Brussels Sprouts over Winter Squash

Serves 4

Brussels sprouts are one of those vegetables that many people learned to hate at an early age. I hear many new CSA members who want to just skip the brussels sprouts, but our veteran CSA members start asking for them early in the fall. I tell the new people that they can't say they don't like brussels sprouts until they don't like locally grown brussels sprouts.

Preheat the oven to 350 degrees.

Slice in half top to bottom and remove the seeds from:

> **1 large winter squash, like buttercup, butternut, or kabocha**

Oil a baking dish or cookie sheet and place the squash on it, split sides down. Place in the oven and bake for 30 minutes.

Oil a second baking dish. Place in the dish:

> **4 pork chops**

Season the chops with a sprinkle of:

> **salt**
> **freshly ground black pepper**
> **garlic powder**

Flip the chops over and season the other side the same way. Put the pan of chops in the oven when the squash has been baking for 10 minutes and continue to bake, with both the chops and squash in the oven, for another 20 minutes.

To yet one more oiled baking dish, add:

> **1 pound brussels sprouts, washed and sliced in half**
> **¼ cup olive oil**

Toss and sprinkle the sprouts with plenty of:

> **coarse salt**

When the squash has been in for a total of 30 minutes, flip it so it is cut side up and return to the oven. Flip the pork chops and return to the oven. Put the brussel sprouts in and bake everything for another 30 minutes, stirring the brussel sprouts occasionally. Remove everything from the oven.

Scrape the flesh of the squash out of the shell into a large mixing bowl and mash. Place about 1 cup of squash on each of 4 plates and spread it around into a disk shape that is just barely larger than the pork chops. Top the squash with a pork chop, and top each pork chop with one quarter of the brussel sprouts. Top it all with:

> **freshly ground black pepper**

Sausage-stuffed Squash

Serves 4

This is an easy way to turn a winter squash into a meal. It's best with a small, really sweet squash like a delicata, sweet dumpling, or acorn. You make individual servings in each squash half.

Preheat the oven to 350 degrees. Cut in half, remove seeds, and place upside down in a shallow baking dish:

2 small squash

Fill the baking dish with water, 1/2-inch deep. Bake for 20 minutes and flip each piece right side up. Bake for an additional 20 minutes.

Fry in a large frying pan over medium heat:

1 pound sweet Italian sausage, casing removed and meat crumbled

When the sausage is cooked, pour off any excess fat and add:

8 to 10 ounces button mushrooms, dirt brushed off and diced

1/2 medium onion, diced

Cook until the onion is translucent and the mushroom is just beginning to look moist, about 5 minutes.

Stir in:

1 cup Italian seasoned breadcrumbs

Remove the squash from the oven and put 1/4 of the stuffing in each squash half. Top the stuffing in each squash with:

1 tablespoon butter, thinly sliced

Bake for an additional 20 minutes and serve.

Baked Fish with Celery

Serves 2

We had a lot of celery for the CSA one year and people asked for more recipes. This ended up being a real favorite. It's a take on the classic lemon and butter fish preparation, and the addition of celery really adds to the fish, and gives you a vegetable at your meal without having to use another pan. Good food with fewer dishes to wash always wins in my house!

Wash, remove stem, wash again between stalks, and slice on the diagonal:

> **2 to 3 stalks celery, leaves and all**

Melt over medium heat in a large frying pan:

> **1 tablespoon butter**

Add the celery and sauté for a few minutes until it just begins to soften. Remove the celery from the pan. On high heat, melt:

> **2 tablespoons butter**

Quickly sprinkle on:

> **2 tablespoons Italian seasoned breadcrumbs**

And top with:

> **12 ounces filleted white fish like hake, haddock, or pollock**

Pour on top:

> **1 tablespoon olive oil**

Sprinkle on top of the oil:

> **2 tablespoons Italian seasoned breadcrumbs**
> **juice of one lemon**

Add the celery to the pan around the outsides, between the fish and the pan. Put the pan under the broiler for 4 to 7 minutes, until the fish is just flaky throughout.

fall | desserts

Pumpkin Cheesecake

This is a cheesecake with pumpkin pie flavor. The ginger snap crust is a great addition, but this can be done with a store-bought graham cracker crust to save time. This is another one of those recipes that my family requests on a regular basis, and seriously, pumpkin pie flavor in a cheesecake? Who wouldn't request it?

Preheat the oven to 350 degrees. Make the crust by combining in a food processor until crumbs:

> **8 ounces ginger snaps (about 1 1/2 cups of crumbs)**

Pour slowly into the food processor, while processing:

> **1/2 cup (1/4 pound) melted butter**

Press the crust into a pie plate. Wipe any remaining crumbs out of the food processor and combine in it:

> **two (8-ounce) packages cream cheese**
>
> **1/2 cup sugar**

Blend until smooth. Add, one at a time, blending until smooth after each addition:

> **3 eggs**

Remove 1 cup of this mixture and set aside. Add to the remaining batter in the food processor, blending until smooth:

> **1/4 cup sugar**
>
> **1 teaspoon vanilla**
>
> **3/4 teaspoon ground cinnamon**
>
> **1/4 teaspoon ground nutmeg**
>
> **1 cup Pumpkin Puree** *(page 152)*

Alternate layers of pumpkin mix and reserved mix into the crust. Use a butter knife to slice through and create a marbled effect. Bake for 55 minutes, until a knife stuck in the center comes out clean. Chill completely and serve.

Green Tomato Mincemeat Pie

This recipe from my mom, Betty, uses green tomatoes as the base instead of the traditional meat or fruit. If you've never had it you may find it to be an unusual taste, but it's something that you'll look forward to at the holidays. The only problem with this recipe is that it takes several days to make it properly—make sure you read it through first before you begin.

In a large bowl, layer:

> 1½ **cups green tomatoes, thinly sliced (about 3 to 4 tomatoes)**
> ⅛ **cup salt**

Cover and let set overnight at room temperature.

The next day, rinse the tomatoes with cold water and drain well. Chop them and put them in a medium saucepan over medium heat with:

> 1 **large apple, cored and chopped small, but unpeeled**
> 1 **small orange, chopped small, seeds removed, but unpeeled**
> 1¼ **cup raisins**
> ½ **cup sugar**
> 1 **cup dark corn syrup**
> 1 **tablespoon ground cinnamon**
> 1 **teaspoon ground ginger**
> 1 **teaspoon ground cloves**

Cover and simmer for 45 minutes, then uncover and simmer over very low heat for 1 to 1½ hours, stirring frequently to avoid burning or sticking. Stop when the mincemeat is thickened. This can be stored, tightly covered, in the refrigerator or freezer if you want to make the filling ahead of time.

Put the mincemeat in a medium bowl. Mix in:

> ¼ **cup rum**

Cover and let the mincemeat marinate in rum overnight at room temperature.

The next day, preheat the oven to 425 degrees. Make one recipe of Basic Pie Crust (page 155), or thaw 2 pie crust sheets from a pre-made package. Roll out half the dough and place in the pie shell, and add the filling.

Roll out the other half of the dough, and place on top. With a knife, trim the edge of the dough to even with the pie plate. Dip your fingers in water and wet the edge of the lower pie crust. Flute the edge of the top and bottom layer. The water will help the crust to stick together. Poke holes in the top crust and brush it with milk to brown the crust. Bake for 40 to 50 minutes. Serve topped with Fresh Whipped Cream (page 158).

Pumpkin Bread

Makes 2 loaves

This is a real treat, especially if served with honey butter to top it. You can serve this at breakfast as well as serving it for dessert. It also freezes well, so you can make some ahead and just pull it out of the freezer and thaw it in time to serve, which is always the easiest way to get ready for guests!

Preheat the oven to 350 degrees. Cream together in a large bowl:

2 1/2 **cups sugar**
2/3 **cup butter**

Blend in:

4 eggs

Add and mix:

2 cups Pumpkin Puree *(page 152)*
2/3 **cup water**

In a separate large bowl, sift together:

3 1/2 **cups flour (white flour or up to half whole-wheat flour)**
1/2 **teaspoon baking powder**
2 teaspoons baking soda
1 1/2 **teaspoons salt**
1 teaspoon ground cinnamon

Add the dry ingredients to the wet ingredients and mix. If desired, add:

1 cup raisins

Bake in two greased and floured loaf pans for 1 hour until the top pops back when touched and the bread slightly pulls away from the sides of the pan. A toothpick stuck in the middle should come out clean.

In a small bowl, mix together equal parts:

honey
butter

Serve the honey butter as a topping for the pumpkin bread.

Pumpkin Whoopie Pies

Makes 24

Who doesn't love a whoopie pie? I'm pretty sure that making them with a vegetable (pumpkin) doesn't even begin to make them "healthy," but it does make a fabulous variation. This one is courtesy of our CSA member Shari Broder.

With an electric mixer, beat together until blended:

¾ cup packed light brown sugar

¾ cup sugar

6 tablespoons unsalted butter

Gradually beat in:

½ cup vegetable oil

Add one at a time, beating between each addition:

3 large eggs

Beat in:

2 cups Pumpkin Puree *(page 152)*

In a separate large bowl, sift together:

2 cups white flour

1 cup whole-wheat pastry flour

2 teaspoons ground cinnamon

1½ teaspoons baking powder

1½ teaspoons baking soda

¾ teaspoon salt

¾ teaspoon ground nutmeg

¾ teaspoon ground allspice

In a third small bowl, mix together:

½ cup sour cream

3 tablespoons milk

Add half of the dry ingredients into the electric mixer bowl and mix well. Add the sour cream and milk mixture and mix well. Add the second half of the dry ingredients. Cover the batter and chill for 1 hour.

Preheat the oven to 350 degrees.

Line two cookie sheets with baking parchment. Spoon the batter onto the baking sheet to make the cakes. Use about one heaping tablespoonful for small pies, or two heaping tablespoonfuls for large ones. Leave some space between the pies as you put them on the pans. The batter may not all fit on the two sheets, in which case you'll need to do this a second time with the remaining batter. Remember, you need two cake pieces per pie. Let the batter stand on the cookie sheets for 10 minutes.

Set the racks in the oven so that one is ⅓ of the way down from the top and the other is ⅓ of the way up from the bottom.

Bake the cakes for about 11 minutes for small pies or 16 to 20 minutes for larger pies, switching the sheets to the opposite racks halfway through baking. They are done when a toothpick stuck in the center comes out clean. Cool the cakes completely on the cookie sheets on a rack. Gently remove the cakes from the parchment.

In a clean bowl, beat with an electric mixer on low to medium speed until smooth:

½ cup unsalted butter
one (8-ounce) package cream cheese

Blend in:

½ teaspoon vanilla
½ teaspoon maple extract

With the mixer on low speed, add slowly and mix until smooth:

3 cups sifted powdered sugar

Once the powdered sugar is fully incorporated, mix at high speed for about 3 minutes to incorporate some air into the filling. Spoon 1 to 2 tablespoons of filling onto the flat side of a cake. Top with another cake, flat side down. Repeat with the remaining cakes and filling. These can be made ahead and stored in a single layer in an airtight container in the refrigerator for up to a week, if you can resist them for that long!

Chocolate Beet Cake

When I started brainstorming recipes for this cookbook, I was a little disappointed because a true local foods cookbook really couldn't include a chocolate cake recipe. Then Abby Harmon, executive chef and owner of Caiola's restaurant in Portland and sous chef, Mike DeLosse, came through with this beet cake, which is outrageously good. Hooray for chocolate beet cake! This recipe actually uses the water in which you cook the beets, so you'll have a pound of cooked beets to serve separately or use in other recipes.

Preheat the oven to 250 degrees. Wash, peel, and grate:

> 1 medium beet

Place a piece of parchment paper on a cookie sheet and arrange the grated beet in a single layer on the paper. Bake until the gratings are dried, 30 to 45 minutes.

Wash, peel, and thinly slice:

> 1 pound of red beets

Put the beets in a pan with:

> 1¹/₂ cups water

Bring to a boil and simmer for 20 minutes until the beets are tender.

Remove the beets. Add water or pour out liquid as necessary to make 1 cup total liquid, and set aside.

Preheat the oven to 350 degrees.

In a large bowl, sift together:

> 2 cups sugar
> 1³/₄ cups sifted flour
> ³/₄ cup cocoa
> 1¹/₂ teaspoons baking powder
> 1¹/₂ teaspoons baking soda
> 1 teaspoon salt

Add and beat with an electric mixer for 2 minutes:

> 1 cup milk
> 2 eggs, beaten
> ¹/₂ cup peanut, safflower, or canola oil
> 2 teaspoons vanilla
> 1 cup reserved beet liquid

Grease and flour two 8-inch round cake pans. Pour the batter into the pans and bake for about 25 minutes, until a toothpick inserted in the center comes out clean. Cool completely before frosting.

In a small saucepan, melt until just beginning to brown:

   1/2 cup (1/4 pound) butter

Put the melted butter in a mixing bowl, and with an electric mixer combine with:

   2/3 cup cocoa

Add, alternating, and mixing until smooth after each addition:

   2 cups powdered sugar, sifted
   1/3 cup milk

Add and mix in:

   1/2 teaspoon vanilla

Beat for 2 minutes or more. One of the most important and often overlooked ingredients in frosting is air, so mix until it's light and fluffy. Frost the cake once cool, and sprinkle the top with grated beets.

Pumpkin Pie

I'm a big fan of pumpkin pie and this is the ultimate spice combination! I had to try a lot of pies to get to this, and I don't regret a minute of it, but this combination really is the best. If you have a spice grinder or mortar and pestle you can have freshly ground cloves, but I would stick with the ground ginger for this because you want it to be fully integrated through the pie; you don't want anyone to bite into a piece of ginger in their pumpkin pie.

Make half of the Basic Pie Crust (page 155) or thaw one sheet of pastry from a package of frozen pie crust.

Preheat the oven to 425 degrees.

Mix together in a large bowl with an electric mixer:

   1 cup sugar
   2 eggs
   1 1/2 cups Pumpkin Puree (page 152)
   2 cups milk or half & half or a combination
   1 1/2 teaspoons ground cinnamon
   1/2 teaspoon ground ginger
   1/2 teaspoon ground cloves

Roll out the pie crust on a floured board. Place the crust in a pie pan. Flute the edges as high as possible so you don't slosh the pumpkin mix as you put the pie in the oven. Pour the pumpkin mix into the pie shell. Bake for 10 minutes, then turn the oven down to 300 degrees. Cook for about 45 minutes until the center is firm. To tell if it's done, stick a knife in the center. It should come out clean.

 Winter

winter | appetizers

Beet and Goat Cheese Dip

Makes about 1 1/2 cups

This is unbelievably easy to make, but don't tell anyone because they are going to be very impressed when you serve it. This recipe has you serve the dip on top of crostini, but it's also a good substitute for humus on a sandwich or wrap, and is a yummy accompaniment for raw vegetables.

Quarter and boil until tender:

    1/2 **pound of beets**

Cool and peel the chunks. Put the beets in a blender or food processor and process. Add to the processor:

    4 to 6 ounces soft goat cheese

Process until it's all mixed. Serve on top of:

    Crostini *(page 156)*

Variations

- Use half soft goat cheese and half cream cheese instead of just goat cheese.
- Use a horseradish–flavored goat cheese.

Root Vegetable Tarts

Serves 8 to 10

These little tarts are fabulous. Whenever I make them for guests I always hope that they won't eat them all so I'll have some the next day as leftovers, but I'm always disappointed. The recipe is courtesy of Brendan Tobin, chef at Aurora Provisions in Portland.

Preheat the oven to 400 degrees.

Dice very small:

> **3 cups mixed root vegetables: carrots, rutabaga, turnips, or parsnips, (about 4 to 6 medium-size root vegetables)**

Place on a cookie sheet and toss with:

> **2 tablespoons olive oil**
> **1 to 2 teaspoons salt**

Roast the vegetables for 15 to 20 minutes until tender.

Meanwhile, make one recipe of Basic Pie Crust *(page 155)*. Roll the dough out on a floured board and cut into circles to fit in mini-muffin pans or other suitable container. Alternatively, you could buy pre-made mini-pie shells in the frozen section of the grocery store. Put a weight in each pie shell, or put another muffin pan on top. This will keep the shape of the empty pie shells. Bake them for 8 to 10 minutes.

When the vegetables are done, put them in a large bowl and mix with:

> **1½ teaspoons fresh herbs, finely chopped**

Place the vegetables and herbs in each pastry shell. In a large measuring cup, mix:

> **¾ cup milk**
> **2 eggs**

Using the measuring cup for easy pouring, pour the milk and egg mixture into the tart shells to near the top of the shell. Top each tart with:

> **1 tablespoon grated cheddar cheese**

Bake until the filling is set, about 15 minutes.

Hot Parsnip, Blue Cheese, and Bacon Hors d'oeuvres

Serves 6 to 8

This can all be prepped ahead, put together shortly before serving, and quickly broiled to make a nice hot appetizer, and hot appetizers are always a nice addition to the party.

Preheat the oven to 400 degrees. Peel and dice into $1/2$-inch chunks:

1 pound parsnips

Place the parsnips in a baking dish and toss with:

2 tablespoons olive oil

Bake until the parsnips are soft, about 45 minutes. Peel and finely dice:

2 tablespoons red onion

Sautée the onion gently in a frying pan until translucent in:

1 teaspoon olive oil

Puree the parsnips and onions in a food processor or blender with:

$1/2$ to $3/4$ cup half & half

Fry in a frying pan over medium heat until crisp:

4 strips bacon

Crumble the bacon and set aside.

Prepare Crostini *(page 156)*.

Up to 2 hours before serving, prepare by spreading about 1 tablespoon of parsnip mixture on each crostini. Top each with a few pieces of crumbled bacon and a few pieces of:

crumbled blue cheese

Place the appetizers on a cookie sheet and broil for 6 to 8 minutes until just hot.

> *Overwintering Parsnips:* You can leave parsnips in the garden all winter and dig them in the spring as soon as the ground thaws and is dry enough to walk on. Get them before they put up much of a shoot. They are a biennial, and as such will begin to make a stiff stalk for seed heads as soon as they wake up in the spring. Once they start this, the root becomes woody and tough and is no longer something you'd want to eat. You will want to be sure you get to them before the deer do.

Goat Cheese Crudités

Serves 6 to 8

Pronounced "crew-di-TAY," it just means raw vegetables, but sounds more highfalutin in French. You can make the goat cheese mix as a dip, or use cake-decorating technique to put the dip on as a topping. They're very cute.

Wash, peel, as needed, and thinly slice:
rutabagas, carrots, and turnips

In a blender or food processor, mix until smooth:
4 ounces herbed soft goat cheese
1½ tablespoons sour cream (or enough to make a smooth but thick consistency)

You can use it as a dip, or decorate the vegetable slices with it. Take a cake-decorating tip (available in the baking aisle of the grocery store). Cut a very small bit of the corner off a Ziploc bag. Stick the tip into the bag and poke it out the corner. Fill the bag with the cheese mix, gently remove the air from the bag, and zip it shut. Arrange the vegetable slices on a plate and squeeze the cheese mix onto the vegetable slices. Top the cheese with a couple pieces of:
sun-dried tomatoes or red onion, finely diced

winter | salads

Parsnip, Dried Cranberry, and Walnut Salad

Serves 4

This is a delightful mix of sweet, sour, and nutty flavors, and looks pretty, too! Even though the vegetable is cooked, it still feels like a delightfully light salad. Parsnips are one of those vegetables that kind of got forgotten over the years. I've given them to people in their 80s who immediately got this happy look of remembrance and said that they hadn't had them since childhood and remembered how good they were. This is a more modern way to rediscover a great vegetable.

Soak 2 hours to overnight, in enough water to cover:

$1/3$ **cup sweetened dried cranberries**

Preheat the oven to 400 degrees. Peel and dice into $1/2$-inch chunks:

1 pound parsnips

Place the parsnips in a baking dish and toss with:

2 tablespoons olive oil

Bake until the parsnips are soft, about 45 minutes.

To make the vinaigrette, pour into a small bowl:

1 tablespoon balsamic vinegar

2 teaspoons sugar

$1/2$ **teaspoon salt**

$1/4$ **teaspoon freshly ground black pepper**

1 teaspoon prepared mustard

Mix with a small whisk. Very, very slowly, whisking all the while, pour in:

3 tablespoons olive oil

Drain the soaked cranberries and mix together in a large bowl with the parsnips, vinaigrette, and:

$1/3$ **cup chopped walnuts**

$1/3$ **cup additional sweetened dried cranberries (not soaked)**

Cover the bowl and chill for at least 3 hours before serving.

Variation

◆ Add $1/3$ cup thinly diced onion on top.

Carrot Slaw

Serves 4

This is a quick, yummy way to serve vegetables, fresh, in the middle of the winter. The Asian flavors come through really well. This might be good served with a nice Thai Curry *(page 38)* with winter vegetables in it. Our CSA member Carol Greenlaw provided this recipe.

In a medium bowl, combine:
   2 tablespoons rice wine vinegar
   1 tablespoon sesame oil
   1/2 teaspoon lime zest
   1 tablespoon fresh lime juice

Add and toss:
   1 pound carrots, peeled and either shaved with a vegetable peeler or grated
   1 small bunch scallions, white and green parts, thinly sliced

Add to taste:
   salt
   freshly ground black pepper

Toss once more and serve.

Beet Salad

Serves 4

Beets and feta are a terrific combination, and the olives in this add just a little more salt to the mix, along with the olive flavor. This is a great recipe to use the beets from the Chocolate Beet Cake *(page 118)*. Now all you need is an entrée!

Boil until tender:
   1 pound beets

Cool. Peel and cut into bite-size chunks. Add:
   1/2 cup mixed olives
   1/2 cup feta cheese
   1/2 small red onion, thinly sliced
   1 tablespoon balsamic vinegar
   2 tablespoons olive oil

Toss and serve.

winter | side dishes

Beet Pancakes

Serves 4

This is certainly not the first thing that comes to mind when you think about cooking beets, but is definitely a good idea. You could also do this with other root vegetables, or make a colorful little plate by making a series of pancakes from different root vegetables. If they are made small enough they can be served as a hot appetizer.

Peel and coarsely grate:

> **2 cups beets**

Toss grated beets in a large bowl with:

> **1/2 medium onion, minced**
> **1/4 cup flour**
> **2 eggs, slightly beaten**

In a large frying pan, heat:

> **1/4 cup olive oil**

Put four equal beet pancakes in the frying pan and flatten them with the back of a spoon. Cook over medium to high heat for about 2 minutes until the pancake is nicely browned. Carefully flip the pancakes and cook for another 2 minutes.

Add, to taste:

> **salt**
> **freshly ground black pepper**

Rutabaga and Bacon

Serves 4

This would work well with lots of different vegetables: parsnip, turnip, carrot, or with stuff like brussels sprouts, broccoli, or cabbage. Flexibility is key when trying to eat local, so make this with whatever you've got!

Peel and thinly slice:
> **1 pound rutabagas (about 3 medium rutabagas)**
> **¼ medium onion**

Heat a medium frying pan on high heat and add:
> **4 slices bacon, cut crosswise into ¼-inch-wide pieces**

Cook the bacon until enough fat comes out of it to coat the bottom of the frying pan, and add the vegetables. Cook over high heat, stirring very frequently as the onion turns translucent, the rutabaga begins to brown, and the bacon crisps at the edges. Turn the heat to medium if the rutabaga becomes too brown. Finish by adding and stirring until the wine evaporates:
> **1½ tablespoons white wine**
> **freshly ground black pepper**

Roasted Root Vegetables

Serves 6

All the root vegetables are tasty when cut up and roasted. I wish my mother had known about this way of cooking root vegetables. The flavors are much better than simply boiling everything. It's not any harder than boiling them, and only takes a little bit longer.

Preheat the oven to 400 degrees. Cut into chunks (smaller chunks will cook more quickly):
> **2 cups root vegetables: beets, carrots, turnips, rutabaga, parsnips, potatoes, individually or mixed (about ¾ pound of vegetables)**

Put them in a baking dish or on a cookie sheet with:
> **2 to 4 tablespoons olive oil**
> **½ teaspoon salt**
> **¼ teaspoon freshly ground black pepper**

Bake anywhere from 25 to 45 minutes. They're done when they're as soft as you like them. Carrots will take about 25 minutes. Beets always seem to take the longest, more like 45 to 60 minutes.

Mashed Carrot and Turnip

Serves 6

Mashed root vegetables are terrific, served with butter and salt. You can mash carrots, turnip, rutabaga, or parsnips, not just potatoes. Here's a combination we learned from my mother-in-law, Lolly. It's a good way to get started with turnips if it's not one of your usual vegetables.

Peel, cut into chunks, and boil until tender:
   $^1/_2$ **pound turnips**
   $^1/_2$ **pound carrots**

Drain and mash with:
   3 tablespoons butter
   $^1/_2$ **teaspoon salt**

Serve topped with a little extra butter and salt to taste.

> ***Storing Carrots and Apples:*** *If you root cellar your harvest, do not keep the apples and carrots in the same storage area. The apples put off ethylene gas and it will turn the carrots bitter. Store them separately.*

Vegetable Gratin

Serves 8

This is a great casserole that you can customize to your liking. It's a good place to start using some root vegetables that you might be less familiar with because you could use a little of something like fennel or rutabaga with more familiar vegetables like beets, carrots, and squash and just get a little taste of new things combined with flavors that you know you like. This recipe comes from David Iovino, owner and executive chef of Blue Spoon restaurant in Portland.

Preheat the oven to 400 degrees. Line a baking dish with:
> olive oil
> Italian seasoned breadcrumbs

Peel and slice to 1/4-inch thick:
> winter vegetables such as parsnips, winter squash, fennel, beet, carrot,
>   rutabaga, or turnip

Layer the vegetables with:
> 2 to 4 teaspoons herbs, such as thyme, rosemary, or oregano

When the dish is half full, sprinkle:
> 3/4 cup grated fontina or Parmesan cheese

Finish layering vegetables and herbs. On the top layer, season with more herbs and pour in just until you see the liquid coming up the sides:
> vegetable or chicken stock

Cover the dish with foil. Bake until all the vegetables are tender, 45 to 60 minutes. Remove the baking dish from the oven and remove the foil. Top the gratin with:
> 3/4 cup grated cheese
> 1/2 to 3/4 cup Italian seasoned breadcrumbs

Bake uncovered until the top is golden, the vegetables are set, and the stock is absorbed, 20 to 30 minutes.

Ultimate Mashed Potatoes

Serves 4 to 8

Did you ever go to a restaurant and have mashed potatoes and you were amazed at how much better they were than the ones you make at home? You probably thought, sure, if I load them with butter and cream they'll be like this at home, but I don't want to eat that all the time. There's actually more to it than that. Here's how to make the perfect mashed potatoes!

Peel:

> 1 to 2 pounds potatoes

Cut them into equal-size pieces and put in a large pan. Cover with cold water to about an inch over the potatoes, bring to a boil, reduce to a simmer, and cook until soft, about 15 to 20 minutes. Drain the potatoes, and then run them through either a food mill or a potato ricer. This turns the potato into tiny little ribbons of potato and that's what gives them the incredible fluffiness you get in a restaurant. Add slowly, mixing with an electric mixer:

> 2 to 4 tablespoons butter
> 1/2 to 1 teaspoon salt
> 1/2 to 1 cup any milk product, anything from skim milk to cream

Taste, and add salt if needed. Use only enough milk to achieve the desired consistency.

Yes, they're better with cream, (what isn't?), but ricing them makes even more of a difference.

winter | entrées

Shepherd's Pie with Rutabagas

I grew up in a family who loved rutabaga and ate it mashed on a regular basis. I understand now that this was not normal, so I get very excited when other people tell me they like rutabaga, especially when our CSA members bring me a rutabaga recipe, and this is a great one from Kris and Ken Konant. Everyone loves Shepherd's Pie, and now you can love it with this imaginative twist that includes rutabagas in the topping.

Preheat the oven to 350 degrees. Peel and cut into chunks:

4 to 6 potatoes
4 to 6 small to medium rutabagas

Place vegetables in a large pan. Cover with cold water to about an inch over the vegetables. Cover the pan and bring to a boil. Simmer until the vegetables are tender, about 20 minutes. When they are cooked, drain the water and set them aside.

In a large frying pan over medium-high heat, brown:

2 pounds ground beef

When ground beef is half way cooked, add:

8 to 10 carrots, peeled and diced
2 onions, peeled and diced
3 garlic cloves, peeled and diced

Turn the heat to medium. Cover and cook, stirring often, until the carrots begin to soften. Add:

2 tablespoons Worcestershire sauce
salt
freshly ground black pepper

Fill a large casserole or baking dish halfway with the meat mixture. Whip the cooked potatoes and rutabagas with an electric mixer, adding:

1/2 to 1 cup milk
1/2 teaspoon salt

Top the casserole dish with the mashed potatoes and rutabaga. Bake for 30 to 45 minutes and serve hot.

Quesadillas with Rutabaga

Serves 4

These quesadillas are really good—the sweetness of the rutabaga is very nice with the heat and the paprika of the chorizo. I served this as samples during our CSA pick up, where I will sometimes hear groans about rutabaga, along with lots of questions about what to do with them. Everyone liked these quesadillas, and yes, most people were surprised. One woman went home and made them for dinner that night!

Peel and cut into chunks:

2 medium rutabagas

Put the rutabaga in a pot, cover with water to about an inch over the rutabagas, bring the water to a boil, and cook the rutabaga until it is very tender. Drain and mash. The smaller the pieces, the quicker they will cook.

Remove from the casing and fry in a large frying pan over medium heat:

1 pound chorizo or hot Italian sausage

Remove the chorizo to a plate. Add to the frying pan:

1 teaspoon olive oil

Place in the frying pan:

1 tortilla

Smear the tortilla with a layer of mashed rutabaga, sprinkle on some of the chorizo, and top with:

grated Monterey Jack or cheddar cheese
another tortilla

When the bottom tortilla is lightly browned, flip it all and brown the second tortilla. Remove from the pan and slice into wedges. Top each wedge with a small dollop of:

sour cream

Variation

♦ For a vegetarian option, use a very thin layer of refried beans instead of the chorizo and use pepper jack cheese to get the heat.

Beef Stew

Serves 6

The trick to a good beef stew is to make a good gravy, including red wine, beef broth, and tomatoes. This gives it enough different flavors to be interesting and delicious. Whatever you do, do not substitute water for beef stock like I used to do. You miss out on a lot of flavor. It is best to eat this stew with Biscuits *(page 156)* so you can sop up all the deliciousness.

Place in a bowl:
- ½ **cup flour**
- ½ **teaspoon salt**
- ¼ **teaspoon freshly ground black pepper**

Heat in a large pan over high heat:
- **3 tablespoons olive oil**

Dredge in the flour and add to the frying pan:
- **2 pounds stew beef, cut into bite-size chunks**

Brown it on all sides. Add:
- **3 to 4 garlic cloves, chopped**

Stir fry for a minute or two, then add:
- **4 to 6 plum tomatoes, diced small or one (28-ounce) can diced tomatoes**
- **1 cup red wine**
- **2 cups beef stock**
- **1 teaspoon salt**

Bring this to a boil and then let it simmer for 45 minutes to cook the stew beef and reduce the liquids, which concentrates the flavors. After the beef has cooked, add:
- ½ **teaspoon freshly ground black pepper**
- **1 teaspoon thyme**
- ½ **teaspoon rosemary**
- **2 to 3 cups chopped vegetables: onions, potatoes, carrots, turnips, rutabagas, and/or parsnips, about 1 pound total**

Return the stew to a boil and then simmer, covered, until the vegetables are tender, about 30 minutes. If the stew gets too dry or you like a thinner gravy, you can add more beef stock or wine to get the consistency you prefer.

Variation
• Add ½ to 1 can of tomato paste to make a thicker gravy.

Chicken with Dumplings

Serves 6

There's nothing like diving into a half spoonful of dumpling with a half spoonful of delicious chicken stew with lots of vegetables. It warms you up just to think of it! This is the perfect winter's night meal.

Cut into parts:

one (3- to 4-pound) chicken, or use 6 to 8 of your favorite pre-cut chicken parts

Put the chicken in a large pot and cover with:

chicken stock

Bring the stock to a boil, turn the heat down, and simmer for 20 minutes. Add:

3 to 4 cups of your choice of chopped carrots, celery, onions, turnips, rutabaga, potatoes, and parsnips, about 1 to 1½ pounds

2 teaspoons thyme

½ teaspoon rosemary

1 tablespoon salt

½ teaspoon freshly ground black pepper

Bring to a boil again, then reduce to a simmer. Cook for approximately 20 minutes until the vegetables are just starting to get tender. In a bowl, combine:

1 cup flour

2 teaspoons baking powder

½ teaspoon salt

In a small bowl, mix together:

⅓ cup milk

1 egg

Stir the liquids into the flour until it is just mixed. Drop the dumpling batter by the spoonful onto the top of the chicken stew. Cover the stew and dumplings and simmer for 20 minutes without lifting the cover. Serve as soon as the dumplings are done.

Savoy Cabbage Soup

Serves 4

"Savoy" means crinkly leaves, so you'll see it referring to cabbage or spinach if the leaves aren't smooth. Cabbage stores well for a long time through the winter. I have cabbage recipes in the summer, fall, and winter sections because cabbage is available for so much of the year. Try this soup from our CSA member Dave Dufour anytime with either savoy or regular cabbage.

Heat in a large pan:
> 2 tablespoons olive oil
> 3 tablespoons butter

When the butter is melted, add:
> 1 medium onion, finely chopped
> 5 carrots, peeled and finely chopped
> 4 garlic cloves, finely chopped

Sauté the vegetables gently until they start to become soft and translucent, about 5 minutes. Add:
> 1 small savoy cabbage, cored and thinly shredded (4 to 5 cups)

Stir frequently until the cabbage starts to wilt, 3 to 5 minutes. Add:
> salt
> freshly ground black pepper
> 6 cups chicken broth

Simmer covered for about 45 minutes. Meanwhile, fry in a large frying pan over medium-high heat:
> 1 pound sausage, sweet Italian, hot Italian, or chorizo

When the sausage is cooked, cut it into ¾-inch chunks. When the cabbage is fully soft, add the sausage to the soup. Return the soup to a simmer, then add:
> ⅔ cup long-grain rice

Cook, covered, until the rice is done, about 15 minutes. Add water if a thinner soup is desired, return to a simmer, and serve, topped to taste with:
> freshly grated Parmesan cheese
> freshly ground black pepper

Authentic Stuffed Cabbage

Serves 6

Ah, stuffed cabbage. If you have any relatives from eastern Europe, you've probably had stuffed cabbage. My Polish mother-in-law calls them *golompki*, my Hungarian aunt calls them *halupky*, and my Russian friend Tatyana Perveyeva Herron and her mother call them *golubtsy*. They are all ground meat and rice wrapped in cabbage leaf, cooked in a tomato sauce, and they are a much loved meal in those families. This recipe comes from Tatyana's mother in Russia.

Wash in cold water:

leaves from one large cabbage

Cut off the tough bottom of each leaf. Boil the leaves for 5 to 7 minutes in a large pan of salted water.

In a bowl, mix:

1½ pounds ground beef
½ cup cooked rice
1 tablespoon minced parsley
1 egg
1 teaspoon salt
½ teaspoon freshly ground black pepper

Heat a medium frying pan and melt over medium heat:

1 tablespoon butter

Fry in the butter:

1 small onion, chopped

Add the onion to the meat mixture. Put 2 to 3 tablespoons of meat mixture into each cabbage leaf, fold in the sides, and roll it up. In the same pan, melt:

4 tablespoons butter

Brown the cabbage wraps on both sides for 10 to 15 minutes, being careful not to burn them. Add more butter if needed to prevent burning. Remove the wraps. In a medium bowl, combine and blend:

3 tablespoons Tomato Sauce *(page 153)* **or canned tomato sauce**
¾ to 1 cup sour cream
½ cup beef broth

Add the pan juices to the sauce and broth mixture and season to taste with additional:

salt
freshly ground black pepper

Melt in the frying pan:
  1 tablespoon butter

Add and blend in:
  1 tablespoon flour

Whisk in the sour cream mixture and simmer until smooth. Return cabbage wraps to the pan and simmer in the sauce for 40 minutes.

Variations

♦ Leave out the flour in the tomato/sour cream sauce for a thinner sauce.

♦ Instead of simmering on the stove, you can bake the stuffed cabbage in a covered baking dish at 325 degrees for 1½ hours. You can serve each wrap with a dollop of sour cream.

♦ My mother-in-law bakes them in tomato soup. Line a greased casserole with small cabbage leaves. Place the stuffed cabbage in the casserole and top with more cabbage leaves if you have any left. Pour one can of tomato soup that has been diluted with ½ can of water over the cabbage rolls. Cover casserole and bake for 1½ hours.

Sausage and Root Vegetables

Serves 4

This one can be different every time, or the same every time, depending on which vegetables you add. This is a great "clean out the refrigerator recipe," but no one will know that's what you did. Our family has been making this for years, and my husband and I would happily eat it once a week.

Cut into chunks and fry over medium-high heat in a large, deep, frying pan:
  1 pound kielbasa or sweet Italian sausage

Add a mix of:
  3 to 4 cups total of onions, peppers, potatoes, turnips, carrots, parsnips,
  rutabaga, winter squash or sweet potato, all cut into bite-size chunks.
  (1 to 1½ pounds of vegetables)

Season with:
  salt
  freshly ground pepper

Cover and continue to cook over low heat, stirring often so that it doesn't stick. Cook until the vegetables are soft and serve.

Pot Roast

Serves 6 to 8

Pot roast is something your mom used to make, and may have fallen off your regular repertoire. Try this version from Jeff Landry, executive chef and owner of The Farmer's Table in Portland, and you'll probably find yourself eating pot roast a lot more often.

Heat over high heat in a Dutch oven or deep, heavy pan:

    2 tablespoons olive oil

Place in the pan and brown on both sides, about 4 to 6 minutes per side:

    one (3- to 4-pound) chuck roast

When the meat is browned, add:

    2 cups beef stock
    one (12-ounce) can tomato puree
    4 ounces mushrooms, sliced
    1 cup heavy cream
    1 tablespoon salt
    1 medium onion, diced
    1 tablespoon Worcestershire sauce
    2 tablespoons brown sugar
    1/2 teaspoon dry mustard

Simmer over low heat until the meat is almost fork tender, about 1 1/2 hours. Add:

    1 cup cubed carrots
    1 cup cubed parsnips
    1 cup cubed turnip
    8 small fingerling potatoes

Continue to simmer for about 1/2 hour. Remove the meat and vegetables to a serving dish and reduce the liquid over medium heat until it is at the desired thickness. Taste the liquid and adjust if necessary with more:

    salt
    freshly ground black pepper

Add the liquid to the serving dish, or serve on the side.

Potato Goulash

Serves 4 to 6

Aroostook County is a beautiful place, and whenever I drive around there I feel like I'm on the top of the world. Potatoes are king there, and people understand that "the industry" (potato farming) is important to everyone. It's big farms growing potatoes as a commodity rather than for sale at a farm stand, but it's a big part of our Maine heritage. Kim Hemphill's husband, father, and father-in-law all grow potatoes in Aroostook County. Her oldest son can't wait to finish school and start farming with his dad. This recipe is from Kim's mother-in-law, Diane Hemphill, who made it often for her grandsons. They loved it.

Over medium-high heat, in a large frying pan, fry:

8 ounces bacon

Once crispy, remove the bacon and drain off most of the fat. Brown:

1 medium onion, chopped

When the onion has browned, add:

6 cups peeled and roughly chopped potatoes

1 cup water

2 teaspoons paprika

1½ teaspoons vinegar

½ teaspoon salt

1 pound sausage or hot dogs, sliced

Simmer 30 to 40 minutes until the potatoes are done. Crumble the bacon into the pan, stir, and serve.

Baked Beans

Serves 8

Many local farmers are adding dry beans to their list of offerings. There once was a thriving dry bean industry here in Maine, which is why we have the B&M bean factory in Portland—it was located close to the raw materials. B&M Baked Beans are good, but if you make your own you get to smell them baking for a couple hours! Be sure to allow enough time to soak these beans overnight. Many health food stores carry blackstrap molasses. If you use this type you will have a much stronger molasses flavor to the beans than if you use other types of molasses, so be sure to choose based on how much you like the flavor of molasses.

Put in a medium bowl:
- 1 pound dry beans
- 1 tablespoon vinegar

Fill the bowl with water to more than cover the beans and let set overnight. The vinegar helps to break down the enzymes in the beans. The next day, drain the beans, put them in a large saucepan, and cover to 1-inch deep with water. Add:
- 1/2 pound salt pork, cut into 4 strips

Bring the beans to a boil, turn down the heat, and simmer until tender, about 2 hours. Drain the cooking liquid into a bowl and put the beans and salt pork into a bean pot or casserole. It's important that the beans are as tender as you want them before you add the salt and sugar. Salt and sugar will stabilize the beans to whatever softness they are at. Preheat the oven to 325 degrees. Add and mix:
- 1 teaspoon salt
- 1/2 teaspoon freshly ground black pepper
- 1 teaspoon dry mustard or 1 tablespoon prepared mustard
- 1/2 medium onion, very finely diced
- 3 tablespoons ketchup
- 1/4 teaspoon paprika
- 1 cup brown sugar
- 1/2 cup molasses

Pour in some of the reserved bean liquid until it's just even with the top of the beans. Bake, uncovered for 2 two hours, adding additional bean liquid to keep the moisture at the top of the beans. Top the bean pot with:
- 2 to 3 strips bacon

Continue baking until the bacon is crisp, 30 to 45 minutes.

Cream of Celeriac Soup

Serves 6

Celeriac is a variety of celery that is grown for the root. It takes a long time to grow, so it's not ready until late fall and it stores really well, so it's readily available in the winter. They are rough and may have some root hairs left on, all in all a pretty ugly vegetable, but it makes a delicious soup. Try this recipe from Joshua Mather, owner and executive chef of Joshua's in Wells.

Heat in a large saucepan until shimmering but not burning:

    2 1/2 **tablespoons olive oil**

Add:

    3 **cups celeriac, peeled and chopped into 2-inch pieces (about 1 pound)**
    1/2 **large onion, peeled and chopped into 1- to 2-inch pieces**
    8 **garlic cloves, peeled**
    1 **bay leaf**
    salt
    freshly ground black pepper

Sauté over medium heat for 10 to 15 minutes, being careful not to brown anything too much, a little bit is fine, but too much will make it sweet. Add and bring to a simmer:

    4 **cups chicken stock**
    2 1/2 **cups heavy cream**
    1 1/2 **teaspoons fresh thyme**

Simmer for 45 minutes to an hour, until the celery root is easily pierced with a knife. Check to see if it needs more salt; if you are not sure, it probably needs more. Transfer in batches to a blender and process, removing the center of the blender top and covering it with a kitchen towel to vent the steam as you blend. (Be careful!) Strain through a fine strainer. It is now ready to go. It may be frozen for a later use, or refrigerated for a few days. Garnish with anything from fresh herbs to diced roasted beets.

winter | desserts

Apple Cake

In this cake the apples are a layer on the bottom under a lovely, moist cake. This is a nice dessert, but it's also a good coffee cake, so you might want to make a double recipe so there's enough left over for breakfast.

Preheat the oven to 350 degrees. Butter an 8-inch square pan. Arrange in the bottom of the pan:

  4 apples, peeled, cored, and sliced

Top the apples with:

  1 tablespoon flour
  1 teaspoon butter, thinly sliced

Mix in a medium bowl:

  1/3 cup butter, melted
  3/4 cup packed brown sugar

Mix in, mixing after each addition:

  1 egg
  2/3 cup milk
  1/2 teaspoon cinnamon
  2 teaspoons baking powder
  1/2 teaspoon salt
  1 teaspoon vanilla
  1 1/2 cups flour

Pour the cake topping onto the apples and spread it evenly to the edges of the pan. Bake for 45 minutes or until the center of the cake bounces back when gently poked.

Carrot Cake

I hear people say that they don't like carrot cake, but I can never understand why. This cake is more moist than any other I've ever made, and it makes it very easy to like. Give this recipe a try before you give up on carrot cake. I have it from hard-core carrot cake lovers that this is the best carrot cake recipe.

Preheat the oven to 325 degrees.

Sift together into a large mixing bowl:
>   2 cups sifted flour (so it will be sifted twice)
>   2 teaspoons baking soda
>   2 teaspoons baking powder
>   2 teaspoons ground cinnamon
>   1 teaspoon salt
>   1 3/4 cups sugar

Mix in:
>   3 cups grated carrots (about 1 pound)
>   1 1/3 cups vegetable oil
>   4 eggs, beaten

Bake in two greased and floured 8-inch round pans for 30 minutes, until a toothpick poked in the center comes out clean. Cool for 15 minutes and turn onto wire racks to cool. Cool completely before frosting so the frosting doesn't melt off.

While the cake is cooling, mix together in a large bowl with an electric mixer until the cream cheese is mixed in:
>   2 cups sifted powdered sugar
>   4 ounces (1/2 package) cream cheese

Add and beat until smooth:
>   1 teaspoon vanilla
>   4 tablespoons milk

The longer you beat it the fluffier it becomes. Assemble and frost the cake when it is completely cool.

Apple Crisp

This is an easy dessert that you can toss together quickly and everyone loves. If you need an impromptu dessert, this is a good choice. It's great served warm, so you can just put it in the oven when the rest of dinner is ready to eat and it will be ready to serve when you're done eating. One of my favorite kitchen tools is the little gizmo that you put the apple on and just turn the handle and it peels, cores, and slices the apples for you. This makes any apple dessert a whole lot easier (and more fun) to make. Serve topped with Fresh Whipped Cream *(page 158)*.

Preheat the oven to 350 degrees.

Peel, core, and slice:

6 apples (about 4 cups)

Spread the apples in a buttered 8-inch square baking pan.

Mix in a large bowl:

¾ cup flour
¾ cup brown sugar
1 teaspoon ground cinnamon
¼ teaspoon salt
1 cup oatmeal
½ cup (¼ pound) butter

Sprinkle the topping over apples. Bake for 30 minutes.

Applesauce Cookies

Makes 4 dozen cookies

A surprising, moist little cookie. It doesn't really turn cookies into health food, or provide you with a serving of fruit, but it's a good little cookie nonetheless. Thanks to my mom for this recipe.

Preheat the oven to 375 degrees. In a large bowl, cream together:
> 1/2 **cup (1/4 pound) butter**
> **1 cup sugar**

Mix in:
> **1 cup unsweetened applesauce**

In a separate bowl, sift together:
> **2 cups sifted flour**
> 1/2 **teaspoon salt**
> **1 teaspoon ground cinnamon**
> 3/4 **teaspoon ground cloves**

Add the dry ingredients to the wet ingredients. Add and mix in:
> 1/2 **cup raisins, if desired**

Drop from teaspoon onto a greased cookie sheet. Bake for 12 minutes, until just barely golden.

Apple Cranberry Cake

This is a wonderfully moist cake. You can make it in a ring pan and have a pretty and delicious cake.

Preheat the oven to 350 degrees. In a large mixing bowl, cream together:

1½ cups brown sugar
½ cup vegetable oil

Add and beat well:

2 eggs
1 teaspoon vanilla

Sift together:

2 cups flour
2 teaspoons baking soda
1½ teaspoons ground cinnamon
½ teaspoon ground nutmeg
½ teaspoon salt

Add the dry ingredients to the wet ingredients and mix well. Stir in:

2 cups peeled, cored, and diced apples
2 cups cranberries

Bake in a greased and floured ring pan for 50 to 60 minutes or 9" x 13" pan for 45 to 50 minutes, until a toothpick inserted in the center comes out clean.

Apple Pie

Ahh, apple pie, the ultimate American food. One of the wonderful things about rural areas of America is the tradition of eating pie with your coffee at breakfast. You may be able to get a croissant in the city, but you can get pie in the country! This is my mom Betty's recipe. Pie, it's not just for dessert anymore.

Make one recipe of Basic Pie Crust *(page 155)*, or thaw 2 sheets of frozen dough. Preheat the oven to 450 degrees.

Core, peel, and slice:

> **6 apples (about 4 cups)**

Put them in a large bowl and mix them with:

> **¹/₂ to ³/₄ cup sugar**
> **2 tablespoons flour**
> **1 teaspoon ground cinnamon**
> **¹/₄ teaspoon ground nutmeg**

Roll out half the pastry on a floured board and put in a pie pan. Add the apple mix. Dot the top with:

> **2 tablespoons butter, thinly sliced**

Roll out the second crust and place on top. With a knife, trim the edge of the dough to even with the pie plate. Dip your fingers in water and wet the edge of the lower pie crust. Flute the edge of the top and bottom layer. The water will help the top and bottom crusts to stick together. Poke holes in the top crust and brush it with milk to brown the crust. Bake for 10 minutes, then reduce the oven to 350 degrees and bake for an additional 40 minutes, until the top is a very light golden brown.

Basics

Balsamic Vinaigrette

Pour into a small bowl and mix with a wire whisk:

¼ **cup balsamic vinegar**

1 to 2 **teaspoons sugar**

½ **teaspoon salt**

1 **teaspoon prepared mustard**

Very, very slowly, whisking all the while, pour in:

¾ **cup olive oil**

The prepared mustard helps to bind the vinaigrette so that it won't separate immediately. This makes enough vinaigrette so you'll have some leftovers on hand that will keep in the refrigerator for a few days.

Pumpkin Puree

To turn a big fat pumpkin into the stuff that comes in the can, you need to cut up the pumpkin and remove the stem and seeds. Cook the pumpkin either by simmering it or baking it until tender—maybe 20 to 30 minutes of simmering or 45 minutes of baking at 400 degrees. Remove the insides from the skin and run it through a food processor or buzz it in the blender, or run it through a food mill. This will make it a uniform consistency.

Tomato Sauce

Makes 1 quart

It seems that oven roasting works great for all vegetables, including tomatoes. You can make a really flavorful tomato sauce by oven roasting the tomatoes first.

Preheat the oven to 375 degrees. Put in a glass baking dish (do not use aluminum — the acid of the tomatoes will eat a hole right through it):

   ¹/₄ **cup olive oil**

Cut in half:

   5 pounds tomatoes

Squeeze out the liquid and seeds, then cut into 1- to 2-inch chunks and spread out in the baking dish. Over 30 to 45 minutes, the tomatoes will release a lot of liquid. When you see the tomatoes swimming in liquid, remove the pan and ladle out the liquid into a small heavy-bottomed sauce pan, again, not aluminum or iron, only stainless steel or Teflon. Bring the liquid to a boil on the stove and then simmer it until it is somewhat thickened, or at least cooked down by ¹/₃ to ¹/₂ of the volume. Meanwhile, continue baking the tomatoes until they are a little drier. Keep an eye on them because once they start to get dry they will burn quickly. You really just need to reduce the liquid a little bit more, not totally dry them out.

Take the tomatoes and run them through a food mill to remove the skins and seeds, then stir in the cooked-down liquid, which is loaded with flavor. If you don't have a food mill you can chop the tomatoes in a food processor or blender and then mix in the liquid. It will still have some seeds and the skins this way, but they'll be chopped really small. When the tomatoes are sauce, add to taste:

   salt
   freshly ground black pepper

Variation

◆ Roast several garlic cloves, a chopped onion, a few chopped peppers, and 2 teaspoons of herbs like basil, thyme, or parsley and add to the processed tomatoes for a chunky-style sauce.

Pesto

Makes about 1½ cups

Is there any food more delicious than pesto? I can't begin to count the number of CSA members who tell me how much they and their families love pesto. It freezes incredibly well so you can have enough for the winter. This is an excellent recipe. My daughter in San Francisco called begging that I mail her some because she had tried all the different ones she could find and none were as good as what we make at home.

Process in a food processor or blender:

> **2 to 4 garlic cloves**

Add and process:

> ⅓ **cup nuts (pine nuts are traditional, but almonds are cheaper and the flavor is still excellent)**

Add:

> ½ **cup olive oil**
> ½ **cup grated Parmesan cheese**
> ½ **teaspoon salt**

Add, 1 cup at a time and blending between additions:

> **2 to 3 cups washed and dried basil**

Add a little more olive oil if it doesn't want to process. Adjust to taste by adding more cheese, basil, olive oil, or salt.

Variation

◆ This also works well with arugula, although arugula pesto is not for the faint of heart. I use pecans or walnuts when making arugula pesto instead of almonds because pecans and walnuts have somewhat more flavor than almonds and can do a better job at standing up to the strong flavor of the arugula.

Basil: Everyone loves to have fresh basil, especially if it's in large enough quantities to make some pesto for fresh eating and to store in the freezer. Typically basil plants are grown from seedlings, which is a great way to get some early basil, but basil has those same life span issues as lettuce and mesclun. When setting out basil plants, start some basil seeds next to them, planting the seeds in close lines just like mesclun. When the plants are four to six inches tall you can cut the whole plant and turn it into pesto, stems and all, because it is still nice and tender. When the basil plants that were set out as seedlings start to put out a lot of flowers, rip them out and plant something else in that spot.

Basic Pie Crust

Makes 1 full pie

This makes enough for a top and bottom crust. Don't be intimidated—it really isn't hard. And you'll taste the difference between it and the frozen ones you get at the store. Though, if you're in a pinch, go ahead and opt for convenience. Some days are just too busy, and local eating shouldn't be just for the weekends.

Mix in a large bowl:
> 2 1/4 **cups flour**
> 1/2 **teaspoon salt**

Cut in:
> 2/3 **cup cold lard or butter**

You can measure this by putting 1/3 cup of cold water into a 1 cup measuring cup, then add enough butter or lard to the cup to raise the level of the water to the 1-cup mark. Discard the water and use the butter.

You can cut it the butter by cutting the butter over and over with two knives until it's pea size, or use a pastry blender, or just make the crust in a food processor and process until the butter is pea size.

Slowly mix in until the pastry just starts to stick together:
> 1/3 **cup COLD water**

Don't keep mixing once it forms together. Shape it into two balls (one if it's half a recipe) and let it rest for 15 minutes. It is now ready to use in any recipe that calls for pie crust.

Biscuits

Makes 12 to 20, depending on size

These are so much better than the stuff in the tube, it just isn't even funny. They are also super easy to make. And surprisingly quick! You definitely have time to make these while that stew simmers. Do it once, and you'll never opt for the store-bought kind again!

Preheat the oven to 425 degrees. Mix in a bowl:

>   **2 cups flour**
>   **1/2 teaspoon salt**
>   **4 teaspoons baking powder**

Add:

>   **1/2 cup (1/4 pound) butter**

Cut the butter into the flour mixture with a pastry blender or two knives until the butter is pea size or smaller. You can also do this in a food processor.

Mix in until the dough forms a ball around the fork:

>   **2/3 cup milk**

Don't over mix. Put on a lightly floured board and roll out to about 1/2-inch thick. Cut into rounds with a round cookie cutter, or the top of a glass if all your cookie cutters are shaped like Christmas decorations. Put on an ungreased cookie sheet and bake 15 to 20 minutes, until they are golden.

Crostini

Slice into 1/4- to 3/8-inch thick slices:

>   **1 baguette**

Brush each side with:

>   **olive oil**

Place on a cookie sheet and sprinkle with:

>   **salt**

Bake on the middle rack in the oven for 10 minutes. Flip each and bake an additional 5 minutes, until golden brown. Remove from the tray any crostini that are beginning to brown and place on a towel or paper bag. Put the remaining ones back in the oven for another 5 minutes. Cool all of them completely and place in an airtight container. They can be stored at room temperature for a week.

Pizza Dough

Makes enough for 1 pizza

This dough is good for calzones or pizza or foccacia. The easiest way to make it is in a standing mixer or a food processor, but it can be done by hand and it doesn't take much longer.

Mix together in a large bowl:

> **1 cup hot water (from the tap, not boiling)**
> **1½ teaspoons dry yeast (about ½ packet)**
> **1 teaspoon sugar**
> **1½ teaspoons salt**

Mix in:

> **3 cups flour (you can use all white or 1 cup whole-wheat flour and**
> **2 cups white flour)**

Turn onto a floured board and knead the dough for 3 to 5 minutes. I almost never have time to let it rise, so I usually just proceed. If you have time, coat the sides of a mixing bowl with:

> **1 tablespoon olive oil**

Put the dough in, cover with a kitchen towel, and let rise in a warm place for about 30 minutes. It is done rising when you can stick two fingers in the middle of the dough and it deflates, but it really is OK to use at any point. Punch the dough down with your fist, remove it from the bowl, and roll into a ball. Proceed with the recipe for whatever you're making.

Fresh Whipped Cream

In a large mixing bowl, whip with an electric mixer:

1 cup heavy cream (also sold as whipping cream)

As it whips, add:

2 teaspoons vanilla extract
1 tablespoon sugar, or more to taste

Continue to whip the cream until it makes stiff peaks.

Hollandaise Sauce

Makes 1/2 cups, enough for about 4 poached eggs

This lovely, lemony, buttery sauce is great on asparagus or poached eggs. The goal in making it is to end up with a smooth sauce, not scrambled eggs in butter. Never get it too hot, and it should turn out OK. If it doesn't, it's really not that many ingredients, just try it again, and you'll probably nail it.

In a small saucepan over low heat, melt:

1/4 cup (1/8 pound) butter

Remove from heat and sir in:

2 teaspoons lemon juice
1/8 teaspoon salt
1 tablespoon water

Very slowly, stirring constantly, blend in:

2 egg yolks

Pour over the lucky vegetable and serve.

tips for vegetable storage

One thing about eating local is that the food won't keep like a box of macaroni and cheese. There is an art to getting the longest shelf life—and to preparing the vegetables for consumption. Herewith, a vegetable-by-vegetable guide to getting your produce ready to eat.

First, you are responsible for washing your vegetables. Many of them are washed at the farm, but certainly not all vegetables are washed there, and each item is not washed with the same attention to detail that you can give in your kitchen, so wash your vegetables!

Second, the temperature that vegetables are stored at makes a huge difference in their shelf life. Some are intended to be stored as cold as possible (without freezing) and some prefer warmer temperatures. To increase the storage life of your vegetables, it's good to know the temperature at various places in your refrigerator. You can find a refrigerator thermometer at your local hardware store for under five dollars. Try it at different places in the refrigerator, adjust the temperature as necessary, and re-check, then remember where the coldest places are and make sure you put your greens there. Put the beans and peppers in the warmest spot. Temperature will make a difference, especially on the salad greens. In the list below, assume that the vegetable will store best at 33 degrees unless it is stated otherwise. Find the coldest spot you can to store these vegetables, even if you can't get your refrigerator as low as 33. Anything above 38 degrees will significantly shorten the storage life of most of your vegetables.

Arugula
If it hasn't been washed at all, wash it when you get home. Dry it in a spinner or by tossing it in a clean dish towel until most of the water is gone. Put a paper towel in the bottom of a plastic bag and add the greens. Make sure that you personally have washed and dried the greens before serving.

Asparagus
Think of these like you think of cut flowers: cut a little bit off the stem so that the asparagus stem will be able to take up water. Put it in a glass of cold water and store in the refrigerator. To use, snap the bottoms off wherever they break easily. This lower part is tough and you just want the tender top parts, which should be most of the stalk.

Beets
Store beets in a plastic bag in the refrigerator. To use, wash them and cut off the stem end.

They need to be peeled because the skins have a much more harsh flavor than any of the other root crops. You can do this either before or after they are cooked. The skins tend to slide off easily after cooking.

Beet Greens
Store in the refrigerator, unwashed, in a plastic bag with the air removed. Always wash before using. If your beets greens have small beets on them, they can be cut up and cooked with the beet greens without peeling them.

Bok Choi
Store in the refrigerator, unwashed, in a plastic bag with the air removed. To use, wash carefully to remove any dirt between the stalks. Remove the stem and proceed with the recipe.

Broccoli
Store in the refrigerator, unwashed, in a plastic bag with the air removed. Wash before using. If the stem is particularly long, you may want to cut off the lower portion and discard it. If the stems are used, you may want to start cooking them slightly before the florettes so that everything is done at the same time.

Broccoli Raab
Store in the refrigerator, unwashed, in a plastic bag with the air removed. Wash before using. Snap the stem off where it snaps easily, anything below that level will be tough.

Brussels Sprouts
If you get brussels sprouts on the stalks, store them in the refrigerator that way, wrapped tightly in plastic. Snap the sprouts off the stems to use. Any yellowed or holey leaves should be removed before cooking or before storing loose sprouts. Store loose sprouts in the refrigerator, unwashed, in a plastic bag with the air removed. If you have loose sprouts, trim a little slice off the stem ends before cooking.

Cabbage
There are several different types of cabbage. There's the regular old green cabbage; savoy cabbage, which is a green cabbage with crinkly leaves; red cabbage, which is actually purple; and Napa or Chinese cabbage. Store them all the same, in the refrigerator, unwashed, in a plastic bag with the air removed. Before using, remove any outer leaves that are dried or spotty. Wash the cabbage. The cabbage may be used leaf by leaf for stuffed cabbage, but is usually sliced or grated. To do this, slice the cabbage in half, cut out the core, lay the flat side down on the board, and slice thinly with a chef's knife.

Carrots

Carrots aren't just orange anymore. There are white, cream, pale orange, yellow, red, and purple carrots, all with subtle flavor differences. There are one or two varieties that are much more tasty when cooked, but your farmer should be able to tell you this. Carrots are frequently sold in bunches with the tops on, but there's no real use for the tops. The tops will respirate, removing water from the carrot, so just cut them off and throw them away (or in the compost) before storing them. Store carrots in the refrigerator, wrapped tightly in a plastic bag. To use, wash them and cut off the stem end. It's your choice whether or not to peel them.

Cauliflower

Store in the refrigerator, unwashed, in a plastic bag with the air removed. Wash before using. If the center is particularly large, you may want to cut out the core and discard it. Cauliflower cooks fairly uniformly and can all go in the pan at the same time.

Celeriac

Celeriac is also called celery root. It is not the actual root of a regular celery plant, it's a separate vegetable that has been bred to have a big fat root and not much top, so that it is now grown just for the root. They are very rough on the outside and rather unusual to look at, but they have a great celery flavor. Store in a plastic bag in the refrigerator. To use, wash and peel deeply enough to remove all the peel and any hairy roots that are left.

Celery

Store in a plastic bag in the refrigerator. To use, pull off as many stems as you need and wash each stem, as dirt gets down in the celery. Remove the lower end of the stem and slice the rest as directed. The leaves are completely usable and flavorful.

Chard

Chard comes with a variety of colored stems, each having slight variations on the coloring of the leaves. They can all be used interchangeably in recipes. Store in the refrigerator, unwashed, in a plastic bag with the air removed. Wash before using. Both the stems and the leaves are edible, though they cook at different rates. If you are stir frying, cook the stems for a minute or two before adding the greens so it all gets tender at the same time.

Collards

Store in the refrigerator, unwashed, in a plastic bag with the air removed. Wash before using. The stems may be tough, so you can either cook them a little longer than the greens or discard them.

Corn

Store corn in a plastic bag in the refrigerator. Corn will lose some of its sweetness as it sits. This is because the sugars in the corn will turn to starch, and it depends on the type of the corn how long that will take. My husband's father used to literally start the water boiling on the stove and then go pick the corn. For many corn varieties, those days are over. If your farmer is growing an old-fashioned variety, the corn will have the most corn flavor, but will lose its sweetness quickly. The sugary-enhanced and super-sweet types hold their sweetness for a longer period. The older varieties are becoming less common, so you probably have a couple days to store corn and still enjoy it. Remove the husk and hairs from the corn and cook.

Cucumbers

There are pickling cucumbers, slicing cucumbers, European cucumbers, and white or lemon cucumbers. Picklers are smaller and are called picklers because they are small enough to be pickled whole. Many people prefer picklers for fresh eating because they believe they are crunchier. You can eat all cucumbers fresh, and you can pickle the slicers or the picklers. The wonderful thing about local cucumbers is that they are not waxed like grocery store cucumbers, so it's your choice whether or not you peel them. Cucumbers actually prefer to be stored at a fairly high temperature; 50 to 55 degrees will give them the longest storage. This will probably be hard to find in your kitchen in the summer, so keep the cucumbers in the warmest spot you can find in your refrigerator, or on the counter if you are going to use them in a day or two.

Dry Beans

Store in an airtight container in a cool, dry cupboard. To use, soak the beans overnight in a bowl of water with a tablespoon of vinegar to help break down the enzymes. To cook, pour out the soak water and put the beans in a pan and cover them with water. Bring to a boil and simmer until the beans are completely soft before adding any salt or sugar.

Eggplant

Eggplant come in purple, white, green, striped, Asian, and Mediterranean. All of them can be used interchangeably in recipes, and will have slight flavor differences. Eggplant likes to be stored at 45 to 55 degrees, so find the warmest spot in the refrigerator for them, or on the counter if you are going to use them in a day or two. Storing them too cold will cause them to get brown spots. To use, wash them, cut off the stem, and peel them. Slice them, lightly salt each side, and let them set for 15 to 30 minutes, which will draw the bitterness. Pat them dry with a towel and proceed with the recipe.

Fennel

Store in a plastic bag in the refrigerator. Unless you have plans to use the stalks in a soup stock or recipe, you can remove them and discard before storing the fennel. Those leaves will respirate and pull moisture out of the fennel, and it's hard to find a bag big enough to cover the entire fennel plant. To use, wash and cut off the stem end and the stalks, leaving just the bulb.

Garlic

Garlic is very happy when stored in an open container on the counter. Terra cotta or ceramic garlic keepers work very well and will keep garlic for months. If you want to store it longer than that, store it in a mesh bag in the refrigerator. The whole garlic is called a head. Pull off some of the outer paper and you can pull apart the small cloves. You can peel each clove, or lay the clove down on a board and hit it with the flat side of a large chef's knife to smash it. This breaks the skin and it can be removed easily. Cut off the small stem end and proceed according to the recipe.

Green Beans

This covers all fresh beans: green, wax, purple, romano, pole, bush, and *haricot vert*. Haricot vert are "French" beans, and are thinner, slightly longer, and more intensely flavored than regular green beans. Romano beans are an Italian bean and may have flat pods or may be round, but definitely have a unique and wonderful flavor, slightly different than regular green beans. Wax beans are yellow beans, and also have their own flavor. Purple beans are purple when raw but turn green when cooked. (The amazing color-change bean!) Pole beans grow on long vines that need a pole to climb, and bush beans grow on short bushes. For most varieties, you won't be able to tell pole beans from bush beans when you see them at the farm stand. Store them all in plastic bags in a warmer spot in the refrigerator, about 40 to 45 degrees. Wash just before using them, as extra water on them during storage will promote bad spots. Snap the stem end off. It's your choice whether you leave the pointy growing end on or not. Green beans used to be referred to as "string beans" because there was a tough string that ran from end to end along the curved inside of the bean. Most bean varieties that are grown now have been bred so that they are stringless. If you find an older variety, you may need to remove the string when you remove the stems.

Kale

Store in the refrigerator, unwashed, in a plastic bag with the air removed. Wash before using. The stems may be tough, so you can either cook them a little longer than the greens or discard them.

Leeks

Store in a plastic bag in the refrigerator. To use, wash and remove the stem. Both the white part and the green leaves can be used. Leeks can collect a lot of dirt between the leaves, especially near the base, so they may need to be washed again after slicing to remove the last of it.

Lettuce

Wash the lettuce head if it has not already been washed and set it upside down to drain for a little while. Shake out any remaining water and put the lettuce in a bag with the corners of the bag cut off to allow drainage for any excess water. Store in the refrigerator. To use, pull each leaf off and wash it, especially at the base, because dirt can get stuck in the leaves. Spin the leaves or dry them with a towel.

Melons

Cantaloupe, muskmelon, charentais, honeydew, and many other kinds of melons are available from local farmers. Some types of melons are best ripened on the vine and some ripen better after they are picked. To tell if one is ripe, sniff it at the spot where it was connected to the vine. It will smell like a melon. You can also tap it and see if it sounds hollow, which will happen when it's ready. All melons will continue to ripen further off the vine. They can be stored in the refrigerator, which will slow ripening, or left on the counter to ripen more quickly.

Mesclun

If it hasn't been washed at all, wash it when you get home. Dry it in a spinner or by tossing it in a clean dish towel until most of the water is gone. Put a paper towel in the bottom of a plastic bag and add the greens. Make sure that you personally have washed and dried the greens before serving.

Onions

Store onions in the refrigerator, but do not wrap them in plastic. Many people store them on the counter or in a drawer, but they really will keep longer if refrigerated. To use, slice off the ends and remove the skin. If it's hard to peel, I sometimes slice the skin lengthwise in a couple of places to make it a little easier. To slice, cut the onion in half lengthwise and lay the flat side down so it doesn't roll, then slice with a chef's knife.

Parsnips

Store in a plastic bag in the refrigerator. To use, wash them and cut off the stem end. It's your choice whether or not to peel them.

Peas, Snap Peas, and Shell Peas

Store in a plastic bag in the refrigerator. Shell peas just before using. Wash snap and snow peas before using, and remove the stem end. Some snap and snow peas have a tough string that will come off with the stem end if you pull down the pea along the seam.

Peppers

Store loose or in a perforated plastic bag in a cool place at 40 to 55 degrees. To use, wash and slice the top off the pepper. Remove the stem from the top piece and remove all the seeds and membrane from the center. You can then slice the pepper into strips or rings or chunks. The top is good to use, too. If they are hot peppers, the capsaicin, which is the compound that makes peppers hot, will get on your hands and from there can get on your mouth or eyes if you wipe them before washing your hands. Be careful with hot peppers, and be sure to wash your hands with soap and water after working with them. There is a lot more heat in the seeds than in the flesh of the pepper, so if you want more heat, use the seeds, too.

◆ Freezing Peppers:
Peppers are the easiest vegetable to freeze. If they get ahead of you, or if you bring a lot in from the garden right before the frost, just freeze them and enjoy them throughout the winter. Remove the stem and seeds, cut to desired sizes or shapes, and freeze. You can freeze them on a cookie sheet and put them in a bag when they are frozen. This will help keep the pieces separate so you can take out only what you need.

Potatoes

"New potatoes" refer to potatoes dug in the summer. They have a soft skin that is easily damaged and are generally eaten unpeeled. They prefer to be stored at 50 to 60 degrees, and so can stay on the counter for a short period of time. If left out in the light, the skins will start to photosynthesize and turn green or darken, so they are best kept in a brown paper bag. Do not store in plastic. Storage potatoes are dug in the fall after their foliage has died back. The skins cure and toughen so that they are not as easily damaged. It's up to you whether or not to peel them. They prefer to be stored a little colder, 40 to 50 degrees, so perhaps in a warmer spot in the refrigerator or a cold spot in the mud room. To use potatoes, wash them and remove any bad spots or sprouts. Your choice as to whether or not you peel them in most recipes.

Pumpkins

Pie pumpkins are generally small pumpkins. What's the difference between a "carving" pumpkin and a "pie" pumpkin? Carving pumpkins are larger, not quite as sweet (although not so much that you're likely to use any additional sugar in a pie or bread), and when cooked down they may be slightly more watery than a pie pumpkin. If the carving pumpkin seems too watery to put in a recipe, just let it sit in a sieve for a little while and let some of the water run off before you use it. You can cook or carve any pumpkin. Store at 50 to 60 degrees, or on the counter. Although they are considered a "storage" vegetable, they do not store as long as the root vegetables, so you're best off to plan to use them up by the end of December or early January. To use, wash them, cut and remove the stem and seeds. See Pumpkin Puree *(page 152)* for further instructions.

Radishes

These aren't just red anymore. Try the white, pink, purple, green, or black ones. Some are very hot, so be careful. The leaves are entirely edible, and can be added to a salad or cooked like other greens. Store in a plastic bag in the refrigerator. To use, wash and remove the greens and pointy tip. To use the greens, wash and remove all pieces of the radish from the greens.

Rutabaga

This is sometimes called a yellow turnip. Store in a plastic bag in the refrigerator. To use, wash and cut off the stem and tip. Your choice as to whether to peel it or not.

Scallions or Green Onions

Store in a plastic bag in the refrigerator. To use, wash and slice off the roots. You can use the both the green and white parts.

Spinach

Store in the refrigerator, unwashed, in a plastic bag with the air removed. Wash before using. If you get a savoyed type (crinkly leaves) it will hold more dirt, so be careful while washing. Dry it in a spinner or a towel before using, even if you are going to stir fry it or put it in a dish. The leaves can hold a lot of water that can throw off the liquids content in whatever you're cooking.

Summer Squash

There are lots of different types of summer squashes, including the typical yellow summer squash with a thin neck and a fat body, little round patty pans in yellow, green, or white, whitish green Lebanese squash, and zucchini in green or yellow, and long or round shapes. They are all interchangeable in recipes and are all stored and prepared in the same way. They prefer to be stored a little warmer, 40 to 50 degrees. To use, wash and cut off the stem end and tip. If they have gotten very large and have a lot of seeds, you may want to remove the seeds. In general, try to pick them at a smaller size before the seeds have a chance to develop.

Tomatoes

Tomatoes come in lots of different colors, shapes, and sizes. Plum tomatoes tend to be firmer and consequently cook down more quickly. Many people prefer them as a salad tomato, too. The flavors of the colored tomatoes vary and so it's fun to try them all. Tomatoes should not be stored in the refrigerator unless they are cut or they will get mealy. Store whole tomatoes on the counter. To use, wash and remove the stem.

Turnips

Store in a plastic bag in the refrigerator. To use, wash and cut off the stem and tip. Your choice as to whether or not to peel it.

Winter Squash

There are an amazing number of different types of winter squash. To try to make a little sense out of it all:

- Small, cream and green and sometimes orange stripes, round – Sweet dumpling – very sweet, easy to stuff, doesn't store too long
- Medium size, green, cream, and orange – Carnival – these are one of the longest storing squashes
- Small, cream and green stripes, zeppelin shaped – Delicata - very sweet, easy to stuff, you can eat the skin. It doesn't store too long
- Large, pale yellow, oval – Spaghetti squash – the flesh is stringy like spaghetti. It doesn't store too long
- Medium sized, dark green, acorn shaped with ribs – Acorn squash – the flesh is dark orange and of medium moisture
- Medium sized, dark green with a little slate green nubbin on the end– Buttercup – very sweet and dry
- Slate green, football shaped – Hubbard – these used to be huge, but there are now smaller varieties – medium orange flesh and medium moisture
- Bright orange, tear drop shaped – Red Kuri – sometimes sold by the variety Sunshine. Very dark orange and moist
- Beige, thick neck and enlarged bulb end – Butternut – fine grained flesh, medium orange and medium sweet
- They all like to be stored at 50 to 55 degrees. To use, wash, cut in half lengthwise, remove the stem and seeds.

recipe index

index